London

London

Denise Silvester-Carr
Photographs by Andrew Butler

COLLINS & BROWN

First published in Great Britain in 1991
by Collins & Brown Limited
London House
Great Eastern Wharf, Parkgate Road
London SW11 4NQ

5 7 9 8 6 4

A CIP catalogue record for this book
is available from the British Library

ISBN 1 85585 036 2 (hardback edition)
ISBN 1 85585 148 2 (paperback edition)

Conceived, edited and designed by Collins & Brown Limited
Editorial Director: Gabrielle Townsend
Editor: Sarah Bloxham
Art Director: Roger Bristow
Designer: Ruth Prentice

Filmset by Servis Filmsetting Ltd, Manchester
Reproduction by Columbia Offset (UK) Ltd
Printed and bound in Hong Kong

FRONTISPIECE: *Tower Bridge.*

Contents

Introduction

L ONDON IS A CITY WITH VARIETY. Lovely in an unconventional way, with surprises round every corner, it is a capital which reveals its secrets in the oddest places and displays its magnificence almost reluctantly. Narrow streets meander into triumphal routes; graceful Wren spires peep from between high-tech towers; Georgian terraces reign over leafy squares; Victorian stations parade provincial wealth; and in a royal park a rustic cottage sits at the feet of a mighty government office. There is an inner beauty too: the sensual pleasures of good living and the intellectual stimulation of a vigorous artistic life all contribute to the vitality apparent in London today.

It was this variety that caused Boswell to admit he often amused himself 'thinking how different a place London is to different people'. Called a modern Babylon by Disraeli and the clearing house of the world by Joseph Chamberlain, London has been championed by the innumerable writers and artists who have found inspiration here. Some, like William Morris who exhorted his readers to 'dream of London, small and white and clean', were perhaps looking through a rose-tinted lens; and Dr Johnson, partly in jest, told Boswell the noblest prospect a Scotsman ever sees is the road to London. Others, such as Monet or Wordsworth, captured it in romantic mood, while Canaletto bathed the Westminster of the 1750s in Venetian sunlight.

London is so full of history that the past is almost overwhelming. Walk through a busy commercial quarter and tablets commemorate vanished City churches; or stroll along tree-lined avenues and blue plaques on houses recall where the famous lived or died. Peer down a concrete stairwell near the Tower of London and the defensive Roman wall is laid bare. Glance at a butcher's stall in Leadenhall Market and be told that Samuel Pepys bought 'a leg of beef, a good one, for

LEFT: *Trafalgar Square is part of the Metropolitan Improvements proposed during the Regency, the largest single town plan conceived and completed in London. The overall scheme was devised by John Nash (1752–1835), who intended to surround the square with buildings for the Royal Academy of Arts and other learned societies; only the National Gallery was built. Nash was not responsible for the design of the square, nor did he live to see it named after the famous naval battle. Sir Charles Barry (1795–1860) laid it out on the site of the former royal mews, overcoming the problem of a slope by levelling the central area and placing a terrace with a flight of steps on the north side. The proposal to commemorate Nelson, the victor at Trafalgar, did not arise until 1837, when a letter suggesting the idea appeared in* The Times; *in 1843 the column with its statue was put in position.*

LEFT: *Two great bronze sphinxes guard Cleopatra's Needle on Victoria Embankment. Designed by George Vulliamy, who based them on statues from the reign of Thothmes III, they were placed at the foot of the monument in 1882. The obelisk, one of a pair erected at Heliopolis, c.1450 BC, was a Napoleonic War trophy later presented to Britain by Mohammed Ali, the Turkish Viceroy of Egypt. When the 3,500 year-old, rose-pink granite Needle was unveiled on 12 September 1878, a passer-by is said to have remarked it was 'the oldest thing in London'.*

LEFT: *This mooring on Victoria Embankment is more ornamental than practical: river craft are not allowed to tie up on this stretch of the Thames. Lions are a familiar decorative theme in London. The 'king of beasts' is to be found all over the city, sleeping on buildings, guarding Nelson in Trafalgar Square or lazily watching the world pass by on top of gateposts.*

sixpence' here; or ask for scent in a 260-year-old Jermyn Street shop and watch it being removed from a gleaming mahogany cabinet made for the Great Exhibition. Sit in a theatre and read that Garrick trod a stage on this same site; or sup ale in a riverside inn and know that Shakespeare probably quaffed mead in this spot too.

The past is always present in London. There are museums for everything, but history does not moulder. Renovation and reconstruction go hand in glove to keep today alive for the London of tomorrow. Technologically advanced offices hide behind the preserved façades of other centuries, and the faint remains of a Tudor theatre are conserved beneath a modern riverside building. At Westminster Abbey, thousand-year-old sculptures mix happily with Victorian monuments, and engraved glass panels placed on the west door in 1990 will give future generations a twentieth-century sampler.

One of the confusing aspects of London is that it is a city, but the City is something else. The 'Square Mile', settled by the Romans north of the Thames at London Bridge 2,000 years ago, is the City of London. It is the oldest of thirty-three administrative areas in today's London

LEFT: *The George and Vulture, a restored eighteenth-century public house in St Michael's Court, Cornhill, is one of many London hostelries with Dickens associations. His bill (£11. 0s. 0d.) for treating thirty-four friends to dinner still exists. In* Pickwick Papers, *during the Bardell trial, Mr Pickwick, 'at present suspended in the George and Vulture', was subpoenaed and arrested here. He later returned, after his release. The boundaries of the parishes of St Edmund the King and St Michael run through the bar, once a popular resting place for thirsty young boys 'Beating the Bounds'. This ancient ceremony, which still occasionally takes place, requires the priest and parishioners to walk the boundaries to identify them. Charity school boys were switched with willow wands and bumped into the walls so they would be sure to remember the exact spots.*

LEFT: *The two fountains by Sir Charles Barry that were part of the original plan for Trafalgar Square were subsequently replaced and, after the Second World War, presented to Ottawa. The new, larger basins of Portland stone commemorate two First World War naval men, Admiral Beatty and Admiral Jellicoe. They were designed in 1939 by the architect Sir Edwin Lutyens, who had blue tiles placed on the base to give light and colour to the water. Seventy-five years earlier, Lutyens' godfather, the artist Sir Edwin Landseer, had been responsible for the four bronze lions that guard Nelson's Column. The fountain on the west side was sculpted by Sir Charles Wheeler, and that nearest the Strand (left) by William MacMillan, whose bust of Admiral Beatty is on the nearby wall.*

RIGHT: *Chelsea has many narrow streets with charming terraced houses. In Justice Walk and the surrounding area, they are a happy mixture of different periods and architectural styles. Many famous writers and artists have lived on this Chelsea estate, which was part of Sir Thomas More's garden in the sixteenth century. The village atmosphere has altered little since Leigh Hunt wrote: 'My family moved to a corner in Chelsea where the air was so refreshing and the quiet of the thoroughfares so full of repose, that, although our fortunes were at their worst, and my health almost a piece of them, I felt for some weeks as if I could sit for ever, embalmed in the silence.'*

RIGHT: *The Physic Garden at Chelsea was not the first botanical garden in London but no earlier one now survives. Many rare plants and seeds from here have been dispatched around the world. Those sent in 1732 to James Oglethorpe, a colonist in Georgia, helped to establish America's cotton industry. The rock-garden was made with old stones from the Tower of London and lava rock brought back from Iceland by Sir Joseph Banks, who also contributed plants collected on his voyage with Captain Cook.*

and, ironically, the most modern to look at. The City is the pumping heart of a great commercial metropolis while the royal, political and more visible historic body of London is in Westminster.

Until it was granted the status of a city in 1900, Westminster had for centuries been a borough that stretched from the City boundaries across Covent Garden and along Oxford Street to the West End and Knightsbridge. In the local government reformation of 1965, all this changed. Westminster gained Marylebone and Paddington, and many other former boroughs in inner and outer suburbs were also gathered into enlarged districts managed by elected councils.

This apart, and a few other idiosyncrasies, like a layout which defies logic, odd street names to recall goods once sold there and coy little place signs announcing Bird in Hand Passage or Tweezer's Alley, London is no more of a problem than anywhere else.

This book is principally concerned with the City of London and Westminster before its boundary changes, though we have made occasional forays to the East End, Greenwich or Hampton Court. We

ABOVE: *Francis Russell, the fifth Duke of Bedford (1765–1805), was responsible for the development of Russell Square, where this 1809 statue by Richard Westmacott stands. A pleasure-loving, extravagant companion of the Prince of Wales and Charles James Fox, the young Duke also had a progressive attitude towards farming. He tested new methods of growing crops and raising livestock and was a member of the first Board of Agriculture.*

have rambled round Marylebone, Hampstead, Kensington and Chelsea to look at Nash terraces, village inns and famous houses, and we have tramped across parks, gardens and open heaths, and into forests to record the best of London.

Without dwelling too long on modern London, we have attempted to portray its evolution and development, to show how a population of over 250,000 people in the City and Westminster in 1700 has declined to just over 80,000 in these areas today, thus explaining why the majority of the 6,750,000 modern Londoners live in other more far-flung districts.

We have looked briefly at important state buildings and royal palaces, and sometimes allowed the camera to linger longer than the pen over the splendours of particular churches or stately homes. In a world of electronic wizardry, we have imagined our ancestors going about their business, bargaining and signing contracts in the more convivial surroundings of coffee houses.

We spent many hours amid the glories of the capital, in the parks which William Pitt, Earl of Chatham, described as London's lungs. And if George II's consort, Queen Caroline, is writ large, it is because she, more than anyone else, was responsible for the shape of Hyde Park and Kensington Gardens today. In the same way, the extravagant George IV and his architect John Nash achieve a prominence in the text because their metropolitan improvements have proved an enduring contribution to modern London.

While neither Andrew Butler nor I spent an undue amount of time sampling the pleasures and pastimes of the city, it was a surprise to realize that the leisure hours of Londoners have not drastically altered in a thousand years.

We have chosen to illustrate and mention many of the sights nineteen million visitors came to see in 1990 and included, we hope, a great many places Londoners and tourists alike might otherwise miss. Taking a cue from the Prince of Wales when he wrote that 'buildings with no hint of decoration give neither pleasure nor delight', we paid special attention to statues, pediments and fanlights, sought out street furniture and noted such period felicities as the armada of galleons sailing down The Mall in the guise of lampposts.

RIGHT: *John Stow, a tailor and self-taught historian, was born near St Michael's, Cornhill, on 5 April 1525. A life-long collector of books and friend of leading antiquarians, he spent the early years of his retirement recording his 'native soil'. He visited all the churches, examined the archives of City livery companies, questioned people and recalled stories told to him in childhood by men who remembered Richard III. A Survay [sic] of London was published in 1598, and Stow received the sum of £3. 0s. 0d. and forty free copies for his pains. He died a poor man and was buried at the Church of St Andrew Undershaft where his widow had this marble and alabaster bust erected. Every year on a date near his birthday, a distinguished London authority gives a short address in the presence of the Lord Mayor and City dignitaries, and a new quill is placed in Stow's hand.*

RIGHT: *The Adam brothers of Scotland developed several large plots of land in London, but little remains of their work. Only a fragmentary part of Adelphi, their grand architectural composition south of the Strand, survives. The Royal Society of Arts in John Adam Street is a reminder of the Adelphi's tall terrace which once rose above arched vaults on the river's edge. The house was built between 1772 and 1774 for the Society, which still occupies it. Its aims are proclaimed on the frieze. Almost all the Adams' houses in Portland Place have been replaced, but a number of the large mansions, designed or decorated mainly by Robert Adam for wealthy landowners, are still to be seen in outer London at such places as Kenwood, Osterley Park and Syon.*

RIGHT: *No one is sure if the king who presides over the rose beds in Trinity Church Square, Southwark, is Alfred the Great. But the statue, which dates from the fourteenth century, was important enough to be in Westminster Hall until 1822. Alfred was the son of Aethelwulf, King of England. As a child he had been taken to Rome, where he was anointed by Pope Leo IV in 855. He grew up to be the great Anglo-Saxon legislator who defeated the Danes and laid the foundations of the English navy. During his reign, he encouraged learning and was himself renowned for translating manuscripts. When the square was laid out in 1824, the statue was placed in front of the church which, now redundant, is a rehearsal hall for London's principal orchestras.*

LEFT: *Few London restaurants can boast a clientele as famous as that of the Café Royal, which reached its apogee during the Edwardian era. Daniel Nicolas Thevenon, a French wine merchant, opened the Regent Street café-restaurant in 1865. The imperial 'N' with the surrounding laurel wreath and a crown was intended to commemorate his trading name—Nichols—and not, as some suppose, Napoleon III (whom he loathed). Originally, French artists met at the Café Royal, but were gradually succeeded by a glittering assembly of British artists and writers who gathered round Oscar Wilde. Max Beerbohm, Aubrey Beardsley and Frank Harris, the editor of the* Saturday Review, *were habitués of the Domino Room. Today, the Grill Room partly occupies the site and, with caryatids and mirrors, retains some of the Bohemian flavour of its Wildean days.*

For Andrew, taking the photographs for this book has been a voyage of discovery, and it has given me the opportunity to look at old haunts and find new delights. Andrew was brought up in London but quickly realized that, until he came to record its beauties so spectacularly on camera, he hardly knew it at all. As a young Dublin girl, London was my Mecca, a city I longed to visit with all the fervour of Chekhov's Three Sisters yearning for Moscow. They never reached their beloved city but I came, saw and was conquered by London.

From a list of places I drew up and with suggestions from other people, Andrew Butler and I trawled London, accepting or rejecting locations to be photographed. Sometimes, road works, builders' skips or cars permanently parked near our quarry thwarted plans. Happily, the weather, which can run a repertoire of four seasons in an afternoon, held fair for the best part of the year we spent working on this book, although the annual summer festival of scaffolding and a forest of cranes often made our hearts sink. Andrew netted Greenwich in the one week between builders repairing the roof and painters re-gilding the spires. The Houses of Parliament, swathed in protective polythene for six years, were suddenly unbandaged for a short while. Mansion House, under cover for months, was caught because we knew in good time that restoration was planned. Only the Royal Exchange, shrouded in what is the latest fashion for hiding renovation work—an artist's impression of what it will look like when the builders move out—failed to lift its veil and escaped the lens.

This book is not intended to be a history of London; that would be an impertinence when there are so many authoritative books on a thousand different aspects of this vast capital. Rather, it is a selection of the brightest reflections in a kaleidoscope, an appreciation of a great city that never fails to fascinate, a place that, as Thomas Moore wrote 150 years ago:

Go where we may, rest where we will
Eternal London haunts us still.

DENISE SILVESTER-CARR
London, December 1990

Streets & Squares

I T IS A STRANGE AND eccentric British characteristic that London has been developed piecemeal. Urban planners are a rare breed, seldom sighted since the Romans left. The layout of their capital—a popular hobby with Continental rulers—has not, with few exceptions, greatly concerned England's sovereigns. London is a city built by people whose inherent traits are on view. It is as if a distrust of logic and symmetry has led to compromise and resulted in half-reluctant displays of the finest buildings. Few designs have emerged to achieve an architectural effect. London's lovable qualities are its crazy illogicality, its ability to surprise, its idiosyncratic informality.

London has variety: broad roads, slender alleys, meandering lanes, small courtyards and large leafy squares. It is a city in which four consecutive right turns rarely lead back to the starting point. Had developers down the ages followed the Romans' plan or adopted schemes promoted by seventeenth and eighteenth-century speculators, London might have had the geometry of Madrid, or a gridiron Manhattan in the Square Mile; if John Nash, George IV's architect, had carried his sweeping changes further than the environs of Regent Street, the West End might have had uniform dignity. As it is, London is a city that seems never to have set out to look like a capital, a situation conceivably rooted in the Dark Ages.

To understand the London of today we have to glance at the past. By AD 60, when Tacitus made his first mention of it, London was 'packed with traders and a celebrated centre of commerce.' A year later, after Boudicca's raid in which the Romans and 'friends of Rome [were] massacred, hanged, burned and crucified', there was massive rebuilding. A basilica and forum (running under present-day Leadenhall Market to Cornhill) went up. Streets were laid out; shops and houses

LEFT: The spacious squares of the West End, with their trees, lawns and flowers, contrast with the meandering City streets. Bedford Square in Bloomsbury, 'one of the finest squares in the world' in the opinion of Steen Eiler Rasmussen, the Danish town planner, is unique in its uniformity. Each of the plain terraces has a pedimented, stuccoed house at its centre, and the dark grey brick on the other houses is relieved by Coade stone ornamentation. The square was built in 1775–83 for the trustees of the fifth Duke of Bedford, and remains in the care of the Bedford estate.

LEFT: *London Wall, a defensive wall around the City, was built by the Romans c.AD 120–200. It ran in a semi-circle from the Tower of London to Blackfriars, and was the base of the later medieval and Tudor wall. Roman work visible in the tiny garden at the north entrance to Tower Hill Underpass rises to a level of fourteen and a half feet. The remaining twenty-one and a half feet is medieval stonework. The horizontal lines of flat, red brick tiles were inserted by the Romans to strengthen the wall.*

The statue, probably a late eighteenth-century Italian copy, is thought to be of the Emperor Trajan (AD 98–117), whose successor, the Emperor Hadrian, probably instigated the building of the wall.

LEFT: *Like other narrow City streets, Ironmonger Lane retains its medieval shape. Early in the thirteenth century, the houses were inhabited by men who made and sold iron bars, horseshoes, rods and cart wheels. Thomas à Becket was born in a house on the Cheapside corner in 1119, where his sister later founded a hospital. Part of this was acquired as a livery hall in 1517 by the Mercers' Company, the oldest and, in order of precedence, the first of the City livery companies. After the Reformation, the Mercers' bought the rest of the hospital but this burned down in the Great Fire and its replacement was bombed in 1941. The present hall, dating from 1954–8 and within an office block, contains wood panelling, glass and carvings from previous halls.*

arranged in a formal Roman pattern; the outline of London was drawn. The Thames, bridged c.AD 43, and the great wall, put up to enclose 330 acres, became the boundaries of one of the largest cities in the Roman Empire north of the Alps.

Some 2,000 years later this area has doubled in size (the City now occupies 677 acres, or just under one square mile) and the network of Roman roads has evolved into today's major highways. These ran either south from the Bridge or through five of six City gates and linked London with other cities created by the Romans: the way to Colchester was through Aldgate and on to Old Ford; Watling Street came into London from Dover before branching north along the present Edgware Road to St Albans.

Virtually no archaeological remains or historical records have survived to tell us what happened after the Roman legions left in AD 410, and it has to be assumed that it was in these forgotten centuries that the

RIGHT: *Goodwin's Court, tucked out of sight behind 55–56 St Martin's Lane, is a rare example of London's fast-vanishing alleys. It first appeared on maps at the end of the seventeenth century and is typical of hundreds of little courts and byways that once darted off main roads.*

The old-fashioned, bow-fronted Georgian houses that survive on one side are of a slightly later date. Once they sold comestibles, possibly to such men as William Hogarth and Thomas Chippendale who lived and worked nearby. Today, they are still business premises but, restored and gentrified, commerce now hides behind ruched curtains.

RIGHT: *Fournier Street, outside the City walls in Spitalfields, retains a little early eighteenth-century atmosphere. The French Huguenot emigrés, who came to live there because it was a noted stronghold of non-conformity, brought a respectability and prosperity which can be seen in the decorative doorways on some renovated houses. Many of the householders were weavers and the silk waste was packed into the floor joists to deaden the noise of the looms. Spitalfields became a slum again in the last century and streets like this were in danger of being demolished: preservation orders and restoration work have ensured their future.*

cat's-cradle of alleys was threaded through broad Roman roads. This lost London, and most of the medieval capital too, has been destroyed—by fire, enemy action and by the injection of sewers, gas mains and service cables.

Contemporary documents extend our knowledge of medieval London, telling of streets roughly paved, full of 'pits and loughs, very perilous and noisome' and frequently encumbered with markets, pigsties and wells. In 1274, anticipating a royal visit, the Mayor, Henry le Waleys, ordered the stalls of butchers, fishmongers and others to be removed from Cheapside 'lest any filth should remain in Cheap against the coming of the king [Edward I]'.

By 1300 the names of streets and lanes are recorded. Streets are generally assumed to be earlier than lanes. Certainly they were more important. They led to places of significance, such as London Bridge or the gates, and were called after prominent features or buildings— Thames Street, or Leadenhall Street after the market. Lanes were more numerous and often took their names from secular buildings or churches (for example, Bow Lane after St Mary-le-Bow), though the

largest group bore the family name of men closely associated with them—Basing after the wealthy medieval Basings, Philpot after Sir John Philpot, Mayor in 1378–9. Like streets, lanes also indicated trades or the commodities sold there—Bread, Fish, Lime, Milk Streets; Honey, Ironmonger, Seacoal Lanes.

After the Dissolution of the Monasteries, the number of tenement courtyards and alleys increased dramatically as land that had formerly belonged to the religious orders became crammed with small houses, their upper floors protruding over passageways. It was through this densely-packed City that the Great Fire raged, reducing the wooden-framed houses to 'a ruinous heap'. In two days and two nights in September 1666 around 13,000 buildings were lost.

Within days of the disaster, Christopher Wren and John Evelyn had been to the Palace of Whitehall to discuss their impressive new street plans with Charles II, and down in Somerset Richard Newcourt was engaged on a scheme to create fifty-five uniform parishes, each with a church at the centre of a rectangular 'square'. The King, who had a strong streak of the town-planner, might have realized a long-held

LEFT: Berry Bros & Rudd in St James's Street is a shop typical of many which supplied the nobility living near St James's Palace in the eighteenth century. From 1696, before it became exclusively a wine merchant's, this was a grocery store. The great scales (still in the shop) for measuring tea and spices were pressed into another use c.1765: customers came to be weighed, and losses and gains were recorded in a book. Six members of the royal family used the service as did many statesmen: to have one's name in Berry Bros weight book was almost like being listed in a social register.

LEFT: Pickering Place, a paved courtyard through an archway by the side of Berry Bros, is a surprising contrast after the wide, impressive approach from Piccadilly to St James's Palace; but London was once full of these quaint examples of town planning. The houses were built in 1731 by the enterprising William Pickering. Offering a degree of peace from the noise of horse-drawn carriages, they were favoured by at least one diplomat accredited to the Court of St James. Early in Queen Victoria's reign, and before it joined the Union, the legation of the Republic of Texas was here, a fact commemorated by a plaque.

GVLIELMVS. III.

LEFT: *When Henry Jermyn planned St James's Square, it was his intention that only people acceptable at Court should live in the fine houses. Arabella Churchill and Catherine Sedley, both mistresses of James II, were among these early residents. They looked out on a prospect which has changed. Jermyn's builders had an ornamental circular pond with a railed surround as the square's architectural feature. This was replaced in 1808 by the equestrian statue of James's son-in-law, William III, and the present gardens. By the middle of the century fashionable London was moving west again, to Belgravia. Clubs and commercial premises were creeping into rebuilt houses, and the square, as the magazine* The Builder *observed, was 'losing caste'.*

LEFT: *Queen Anne's Gate, a small street with an elegant ensemble of houses built in 1705, was named after the Stuart Queen whose statue—in a niche by No 15—was placed in the street during her lifetime. The street is all that remains of two adjoining closes on the south side of St James's Park and is a fine example of a fashionable street of the eighteenth and nineteenth centuries which had many important residents. A number of the brown brick houses still have square-headed front doors with elaborate carved wood canopies. The intricate foliage carved on the brackets, pendants and friezes, combined with the sculpted keystones and quoins in contrasting brick, make the houses the best examples of their period in London.*

ambition to build a regal capital had not more urgent commercial considerations prevailed. It was impressed on him that if the City was to survive as a major trading centre it had to be rebuilt quickly. There was also the problem of rebuilding whole streets in one operation: co-ordinating individual landowners was an impossible task, hence the outline of closely-knit streets was retained.

More than a century later, *c.*1770, a German visitor wrote that the City, especially along the banks of the Thames, 'is composed of old ruins: the streets are narrow, obscure and badly paved ... The contrast betwixt that and the western parts of the metropolis is astonishing: the houses there are almost all new ... the squares are magnificent; the streets are built in straight lines ... no city in Europe is better paved.'

The West End seen by Baron Johann Wilhelm von Archenholz was mostly new. From Saxon times London had been gradually expanding beyond the walls. Tiny half-timbered houses huddled on thin streets had multiplied near Westminster Abbey. Across the river, Southwark was a substantial suburb which had a centuries-old past when Henry VIII came to the throne. Little villages like Marylebone had grown up

LEFT: *Like many other squares, Berkeley Square, as Max Beerbohm observed, isn't a true square. And no nightingale has been sighted or heard to sing there. It was developed in the 1730s by the fifth Baron Berkeley, a descendant of Lord Berkeley of Stratton, the royalist commander during the Civil War who acquired the land after the Restoration. Although rebuilt a number of times, several houses surviving on the west side give a suggestion of the square's original flavour. No 44, designed by William Kent, has been described by the architectural historian Sir Nikolaus Pevsner as 'the finest terrace house of London'. Plane trees planted by Mr Bouverie, the neighbour of Horace Walpole (1717–97) who lived and died at No 11, today spread out as a leafy roof over the lawn.*

LEFT: *Grosvenor Square, centrepiece of the Duke of Westminster's great estate in Mayfair, was developed by his ancestor Sir Richard Grosvenor (1689–1732) in the final years of his life. He had inherited the land from his mother, Mary Davies, a young heiress whose 'infinitely rich' great uncle, Hugh Audley, made his fortune during the Commonwealth.*

Sir Richard did not see the completion of the adjacent streets, which were given names connected with the Grosvenor family. Many famous people, including George I's mistress, the Duchess of Kendal, and the letter-writing fourth Earl of Chesterfield, were early residents. The square's long association with the United States of America began when John Adams, later second President, became the first US minister to the Court of St James in 1785.

around churches that served rural communities. Noblemen, courtiers and provincial bishops who attended Court or Parliament had large houses along the Strand. During the Dissolution, these episcopal palaces and church lands were granted to Court favourites or sold to speculative builders. New ownership led to the great honeypot developments Von Archenholz had admired in the West End.

Long Acre, once the convent garden of Westminster Abbey, became the property of the first Earl of Bedford whose great-grandson

BELOW: *Edwardes Square in Kensington was developed between 1811 and 1820 for Lord Kensington, whose family name was Edwardes, and this Greek Revival temple was placed at the entrance to the gardens. When houses were going up, a rumour circulated that the occupants would be officers in Napoleon Bonaparte's invading army, a story which arose simply because the builder's name was French!*

employed Inigo Jones to design a plan for the land north of the Strand. In 1630, inspired by his visits to Italy and possibly by the Place Royale in Paris, Jones created a large, formal, classical piazza, the forerunner of a great many similiar schemes. It was London's first square, though not called so—the first of over 120 in central London today.

Initially, Jones's influence spread only to Lincoln's Inn where the benchers, objecting to a plan to put up houses, wanted to turn three meadows into a place of 'public health and pasture'. Despite their opposition, a compromise was reached and terraces with Palladian façades were set round the railed-off fields. A quarter of a mile away in Bloomsbury, the fourth Earl of Southampton had plans for a town house at the bottom of his Long Field and granted leases on its edges to individual builders. When John Evelyn visited it in 1665, he saw 'a noble square or piazza, a little towne ... a naked garden to the north, but good aire.' Bloomsbury Square (called Southampton originally) was the first square in London to be called a square. Terraced houses of different sizes, with alleys and mews for stables and servants' quarters at the rear, overlooked the central garden; its north side was dominated by Southampton House, and in side streets shops and small businesses—Evelyn's 'little towne'—had been set up.

Something grander was envisaged for St James's by the diplomat Henry St Jermyn. He had a Crown lease on the understanding that houses near the palace were occupied by respectable people. Plots in the square were leased to noblemen or reputable speculators. Secondary streets with shops were laid out. A poultry and meat market stood close to modern Lower Regent Street, and a church, which Jermyn largely paid for, was designed by Sir Christopher Wren. St James's Square, with a large ornamental pond (replaced now by gardens and the statue of William III), became, as Jermyn hoped, the most fashionable district in London. Within fifty years seven dukes, seven earls and two of James II's mistresses had lived there.

Other great landowning families, seeing the advantage of turning their property to account and realizing they could determine what neighbours they had, were quick to seize on the idea of creating a small estate with a community living in or close to a garden square. By the end of the eighteenth century the Cadogans in Chelsea, the Fitzroys at

RIGHT: *This house is in Paultons Square, one of many Chelsea streets and squares associated with the Sloane family and its descendants. Sir Hans Sloane (1660–1753), Court physician, collector and antiquarian, bought Chelsea Manor House (built by Henry VIII) from Charles Cheyne in 1712. The estate passed to his two daughters. The larger share, which went to Elizabeth, Lady Cadogan, forms Earl Cadogan's large holding in present-day Chelsea. Sarah, the wife of George Stanley of Paultons in Hampshire, inherited the land around Beaufort House where a large formal garden had surrounded the beautiful sixteenth-century home of Sir Thomas More. Sloane had bought More's house in 1736 but knocked it down; fortunately, only a market garden was lost when the pleasing late Georgian square was built in the 1830s.*

ABOVE: *South Eaton Place, one of many terraces leading from the squares in Belgravia, was built on part of nineteen acres known as the Five Fields, south of Knightsbridge. Thomas Cubitt (1788–1855), a ship's carpenter turned speculative builder, leased the land from Robert, the second Earl Grosvenor; and from 1825 to 1855 he oversaw a development to rival Mayfair and Regent's Park. Cubitt's street layouts were more regimented than Nash's but his houses are more solid: he employed contractors whose workmanship was sounder.*

Euston, the Grosvenors in Mayfair and the Portmans in Marylebone had built streets of terraced houses leading off squares, and given them names associated with their families: for example, Tavistock, Russell, Bedford, Woburn, on the dukes of Bedford's land in Bloomsbury.

The Georgian squares remain but Bedford Square is the only one to have survived intact. The most consistently uniform, its construction overseen by the fifth Duke's guardians, it was built to attract people of more modest means who, unlike the aristocratic families, did not mind that every house in the square looked almost the same.

Elsewhere in the West End, streets and squares were developed by speculators with less aesthetic considerations, such as Sir Thomas Bond and Colonel Panton. They did not worry very much about projects on adjacent sites or estates, and scant regard was paid to such niceties as alignment. The most notorious amateur speculator was Nicholas Barbon, a rogue who resorted to devious practices and bought up any properties that stood in the way of his schemes. When angry owners had to be placated he arrived at meetings 'as richly dressed as a lord of the bedchamber on a birthday' and 'with mountebank speech … proposed his terms', which coming from a honey-tongued imposter had an air of credibility. He developed Red Lion Square and built houses in Mincing Lane where the vaults fell in 'most scandalously'. His most daring plan was to buy Essex House on the Strand, defying the wishes of Charles II who wanted to grant it to a courtier. He tore up the garden, pulled down the great Tudor mansion and filled Essex Street with 'taverns, alehouses, cookshops and vaulting schools'.

One courtier who did not succumb to the pastoral pleasures of a communal garden was Sir Thomas Neale, the wily Mint Master to William and Mary. He had no intention of losing revenue by wasting space with a tree-filled square for well-to-do residents. On the acquisition of Crown land in a corner of Covent Garden, he chose a Continental notion—a *rond point*. Like the dukes and earls, he wanted a focal point but a small one. He put up an obelisk surmounted by the sundial that gave the district its name, Seven Dials. The narrow, unbending streets that radiated from it eventually fell into disrepair and, like much of adjacent Soho, became packed with unsavoury slums and rookeries.

ABOVE AND RIGHT: *The success of Belgrave Square as a fashionable alternative to the West End was assured when Queen Victoria rented No 36 for her mother, the Duchess of Kent, and then for her son, the Duke of Connaught, and other royals rented houses. The regularity of the square, planned for Cubitt by George Basevi, is relieved by mansions placed diagonally on three corners. Seaford House (right) is the most palatial. The architect Philip Hardwick designed it for Lord Sefton. Since the Second World War, embassies have occupied the houses.*

ABOVE: *Park Crescent is part of an uncompleted plan by John Nash for a processional thoroughfare for the Prince Regent from St James's Park to Regent's Park. He envisaged three circuses—one at the intersection with Piccadilly and one at Oxford Street, while the third and largest was to be the entrance to the new park at Marylebone. It would curve from Portland Place, the street Robert and John Adam had begun in 1774, and lead to a proposed pleasure pavilion for the Prince. Nash's builders went bankrupt and only Park Crescent, half of the Ionic-colonnaded circus, was completed.*

Many dingy Soho streets were swept away early in the nineteenth century in the only important attempt to give London a sense of style. This was the scheme devised by John Nash for the Prince Regent. Nash's wide thoroughfare cut through the West End, demolishing a warren of tenements. Connecting the Prince's Carlton House (pulled down soon after) with Regent's Park, the New Street, as Regent Street was first called, curved past Nash's colonnaded Quadrant. It incorporated the Adam brothers' stately Portland Place by placing All Souls' Langham Place 'like the knee of a jointed doll' on the bend, and progressed into the park by way of a crescent of stuccoed houses. On the park boundaries, Nash supervised the building of majestic terraces.

More Soho slums were cleared away when Shaftesbury Avenue and Charing Cross Road were created in the 1880s, and a few years later a cluster of medieval streets around Drury Lane disappeared with the building of the Aldwych and the Kingsway underpass.

Nash did not live to see his Charing Cross Improvements Scheme develop into Trafalgar Square, nor did he know he was to inspire another large undertaking. This was a joint venture between the second Earl Grosvenor and the builder Thomas Cubitt on reclaimed marshy land in Belgravia and Pimlico. The street plan reflects Cubitt's belief in geometry but the cream mansions set in squares and on wide streets are more solid versions of Nash's romantic crescents and terraces.

Although the appearance of London has greatly changed, its topography, particularly in the City, remains much as intended by the men who laid it out whenever parcels of land were available at various times over 2,000 years. Even after the severe bomb damage of the Second World War, the street plan was never altered, and the same problems encountered after the Fire of London had to be overcome. More recently, the demand for commercial space has resulted in a taller City, a City whose fabric is constantly changing. On the other hand, the streets and meandering lanes have remained, and today's map can be imposed without any great difficulty on a map drawn by a cartographer in *c.*1555. In the younger West End gradual changes have been made to cope with the demands of a modern world and increased traffic. However eccentric its layout, London's streets and squares have an amazing capacity to surprise: they are London's special charm.

RIGHT: *Portland Place, once the widest street in London, has a central island which is ideal for the display of sculpture, though only Lord Lister, Quentin Hogg and Field Marshal Sir George White occupy the long run. John Tweed's bronze, one of numerous equestrian statues in London, shows the Commander-in-Chief of the Indian Army, Sir George White. Like those of many other eighteenth and nineteenth-century military men, the exploits of the much-decorated George Stuart White, a soldier born in Ulster in 1835, are largely forgotten. He was awarded the Victoria Cross for personal gallantry during the Indian Mutiny, and again distinguished himself in South Africa, defending Ladysmith during the Boer War. He died in 1912 at the Royal Hospital, Chelsea, of which he was Governor.*

RIGHT: *Sir Thomas Bond, a follower of Charles II, formed a syndicate to buy the Clarendon estate north of Piccadilly. But he died in 1685, a year before the street that bears his name in the 'new town' was completed. The original street ran as far as Burlington Gardens; the extension to Oxford Street—New Bond Street—was finished in the 1720s. The exclusive shops were patronized by residents of St James's, Mayfair and Belgravia who, wishing to be 'smart', followed such arbiters of fashion as the 'Bond Street Loungers', among them the 'tall and stately galleon', Beau Brummel. Many famous people, such as Lord Nelson, lived in the street, and the home of the actor, Sir Henry Irving, was above Asprey's, the silversmith's and jeweller's founded in 1781 and still flourishing.*

RIGHT: *In Regent Street, John Nash intended that there should be 'room for all the fashionable shops to be assembled in one street.' His favourite project on the 'magnificent thoroughfare' was the Quadrant, a covered walk to protect the gentry on rainy days. Curving north from Piccadilly Circus, the colonnade was removed in 1848, twenty-eight years after its completion, because it had become a 'haunt for vice and immorality'. Nash's stuccoed shops were demolished early this century and replaced with far grander buildings in a style Pevsner called 'Imperialist Baroque'. Several stores of the type envisaged by Nash have survived into this century: Dickins and Jones arrived in Regent Street in 1835, Liberty and Co. in the 1860s and Mappin and Webb in 1872.*

CHAPTER 2

Church & State

T HE INTRICATE RELATIONSHIP between Church and State is not always visible in the face they present to London. Since William the Conqueror was crowned in Westminster Abbey, both estates have been symbolized in their principal London buildings, yet neither sets out to dominate the other architecturally. At Westminster they achieve a harmony which is reflected in each other's grace notes, the Perpendicular fripperies and elegant Early English style of the Abbey complementing the rich Victorian Gothic Revival decoration of the Houses of Parliament.

In practice, the relationship has been more discordant. Since the Reformation, Parliament has legislated on measures proposed by the established Church. This seems paradoxical in a country where today, though the majority of people belong nominally to the Church of England, less than three per cent attend church regularly. In the City, where places of worship outnumber buildings of civic importance, the discrepancy is stranger still. God met Mammon and lost: more than thirty of forty-two churches are closed on Sundays.

Parliament sits at Westminster because William I's successors chose to conduct affairs of state close to the great Benedictine Abbey that Edward the Confessor had built, but the country's most important church is at Canterbury where St Augustine introduced Christianity in the sixth century. Nor is Westminster Abbey London's most important church. It fulfils a valuable role on royal and national occasions, but St Paul's is the capital's principal church, the cathedral church of the diocese and seat of the Bishop of London. The Abbey, however, does not owe allegiance to any bishop, not even to the Archbishop of Canterbury. It is a 'royal peculiar', the Dean and Chapter of which are answerable only to the monarch. A further anomaly is that, though the

BELOW: *This Coade stone lion on Westminster Bridge, put there at the request of George VI, guarded a brewery in Lambeth from 1837 until the Second World War. Heraldic lions appeared on the Second Great Seal of Richard I c.1195 and have been on England's arms ever since.*

LEFT: *The Palace of Westminster, better known as the Houses of Parliament, is a Gothic Revival building designed in the mid-nineteenth century by Sir Charles Barry with intricate decoration by Augustus Welby Pugin. It stands on the site of the royal palace where England's system of government developed. In Westminster Hall, Parliamentary procedures were started when Edward I presided over the Model Parliament of 1295. The House of Lords assembled in the Painted Chamber of the palace and the Commons met nearby in the Chapter House of Westminster Abbey.*

BELOW: *A gargoyle, one of six, juts from the end of the triple gable over the north porch at Westminster Abbey. The statues and foliage were renewed by Victorian craftsmen c.1875–90. In the centre doorway, Christ the King surmounts the twelve apostles, and below is a figure of the Virgin and Child.*

RIGHT: *The north porch is the earliest part of Westminster Abbey, and was the nearest entrance to the kings' palace. Originally of stone quarried at Caen in France and brought to England at great expense, the façade was remodelled in the last century largely by Sir George Gilbert Scott. The rose window between the flying buttresses and above the lancet windows is entirely Scott's work.*

seat of the Primate of All England is at Canterbury, the administrative headquarters of the Church are beside Westminster Abbey: at Church House in Dean's Yard.

The strange relationship between Church and State has evolved from a time seven centuries ago when the Court of the King—an assembly of archbishops, bishops, abbots, priors and up to one hundred secular peers—met at Westminster Palace to parley (hence parliament). This body eventually became the House of Lords and now, in the late twentieth century, it numbers twenty-six spiritual peers and over one thousand hereditary and life peers.

RIGHT: *The Cloisters at Westminster Abbey are contemporary with the oldest parts. The Muniment Room and the thirteenth-century Chapter House, where the House of Commons met for three hundred years, are on the east walk. This circular-shaped assembly room was never returned to the Abbey after its secular use and remains the property of the State. Stone benches line the long openings of the Cloisters overlooking the lawn. On Holy Thursday, people who came to collect Maundy money would have sat on them while their feet were washed, in a ceremony recalling Christ's washing of the apostles' feet. The tracery of the windows and the simple architectural style of the arcades have, in places, been influenced by French cathedrals. On the walls and floors, memorials— some twelfth-century, others very recent—recall significant moments in history, as well as men and women from all walks of life.*

LEFT: *Most Saxon and medieval churches in the City were destroyed in the Great Fire in 1666 but some outside the walls survive. At Smithfield in 1123, Henry I's court jester, Rahere, built a church and a hospital dedicated to St Bartholomew. The hospital, the first in London, has been rebuilt several times but traces of the former Augustinian priory remain. With later additions, it is a good example of Transitional architecture; the difference between the solid Norman arches and pointed Gothic work is visible in the nave. Rahere was buried in the church, but his original tomb was replaced in the fifteenth century. Outside in the churchyard, every Good Friday, coins and hot cross buns were placed on the flat tombstones for 'poor widows of the parish': nowadays children receive this charity.*

LEFT: *Southwark Cathedral is, after Westminster Abbey, London's finest Gothic church. The Bishop of Winchester, whose palace was adjacent, was responsible for the parish until 1897. Inside there is a memorial to William Shakespeare, whose brother Edward was buried here; and a chapel commemorates John Harvard who was baptized here in 1607 before he emigrated to Massachusetts where he founded the university.*

ABOVE: *A rose window with delicate stone tracery, in a wall in Clink Street, is all that remains of the bishops of Winchester's palace. The bishops owned most of the property on the river and collected rents and fines from the brothels whose ladies were nicknamed 'Winchester geese'.*

Commoners who came to petition the king met separately in the Chapter House of Westminster Abbey. Many of these men, often younger sons of noblemen with no great inheritance, put themselves forward for election to Westminster and formed the link between the landed classes and the ordinary people. The bond that united this feudal pyramid of king, lords, commoners and serfs was the Church.

By the time of Henry VIII's accession, the Church had become so powerful that the clergy and laymen under its protection had become divorced from common law. Also, the revenues of more than one hundred churches and a further thirteen large monasteries in or within a mile of the City were remitted to Rome. Their wealth, coupled with propaganda about the lax behaviour of 'priests and clerks in time of divine service [being found] at taverns, ale houses, at fishing and other trifles', led to a great wave of anti-clerical feeling. Combined with Henry's marital disagreement with Rome, this popular disaffection contributed to the Reformation.

During the Dissolution of the Monasteries in 1536, Henry VIII sold many of the London palaces of the spiritual lords to the highest bidder to pay for his wars with France or gave them as rewards to Court favourites. Norwich House was acquired by the Duke of Suffolk. Durham House became the home of Edward VI and little Princess Elizabeth. Carlisle House was leased to Lord Russell. The Lord Protector Somerset built his mansion on the site of the houses of the Bishops of Chester, Llandaff and Worcester; and the house of the Bishop of Bath and Wells eventually became Arundel House, the great town house of the Howard family. Today, one remains—Lambeth Palace, the Archbishop of Canterbury's London residence, safely distanced by the Thames from Westminster.

More recently, the decline of the established Church and in non-conformity has given the monarchy greater significance. This has been particularly apparent this century when the Crown has been seen to impart a moral influence. As Head of State and Defender of the Faith (a title conferred on Henry VIII by Pope Leo X in 1521 for his stand against Luther), the sovereign symbolizes the political and religious lives of the country, and we see these bonds on state occasions when royalty, churchmen and politicians come together for great ceremonials.

ABOVE: *Christopher Wren built fifty-two churches in London after the Great Fire. Almost all had beautiful spires and St Mary le Bow's, with its circular colonnade, is one of the finest. The balustraded balcony above the tower commemorates the royal box on the earlier church. The king sat there to watch jousts in Cheapside in the Middle Ages.*

RIGHT: *Nicholas Hawksmoor, 'domestic clerk' to Wren, began work on Christ Church, Spitalfields, soon after Parliament passed Queen Anne's Act of 1711 for building fifty new churches. The celebrated baroque building, its great Tuscan portico and square tower emphasized by the slender, soaring spire, was intended as one of these. More churches were needed to minister to a fast-growing population in the years after the Great Fire, but in the event only twelve were built—two others in the East End also by Hawksmoor (St Anne's, Limehouse, and St George's in the East). Christ Church served the Huguenot community—mostly silk weavers who had fled from France after Louis XIV revoked the Edict of Nantes in 1685.*

LEFT: *Wren's loveliest spire, on St Bride's, Fleet Street, is said to have been the inspiration for tiered wedding cakes. William Rich (1755–1811), a baker on Ludgate Hill, got the idea from the steeple he could see from his window. The museum in the crypt, which displays a party dress belonging to his wife Susannah, traces the history of the parish through 1,500 years.*

RIGHT: *The Catholic Emancipation Act of 1828 restored to Roman Catholics most religious, civil and political rights denied to them after the Reformation. At the instigation of John Henry Newman, the Oratory (an order of priests founded in Rome in the sixteenth century by St Philip Neri) established a community in London in 1849. They later moved west, and the Italian Renaissance-style Brompton Oratory (the second-largest Catholic church in the capital) was built between 1880 and 1884. Elaborately ornamented outside, the interior is predominantly blue and gold with rich ceiling decoration and side altars which have splendid paintings and statues. The large mosaic figures on the gold background on the spandrels under the dome are the four Evangelists.*

RIGHT: *An inscribed plaque in the porch of the Greek Cathedral of St Sophia, Moscow Road, commemorates an earlier seventeenth-century Greek church in Hog Lane, Soho. This was swept away when the Charing Cross Road was cut through in the 1870s. The dull exterior of the Bayswater replacement, designed by John Oldrid Scott in the form of a Greek cross (and based on St Sophia in Istanbul), gives no hint that the interior of the city's only Greek Cathedral glistens with gold mosaics and icon paintings by Ludwig Thiersch. The great dome and surrounding arches and friezes are lined with angels and evangelists. Pantokrator (Almighty God), at the centre of the dome, is ringed by twelve lunettes interspersed with apostles.*

The most solemn ceremony, and the most religious, is a coronation. Every sovereign from William I in 1066 to Queen Elizabeth II in 1953 (except Edward V and Edward VIII) has been anointed and crowned in Westminster Abbey, latterly vowing to preserve the Church of England. The annual State Opening of Parliament serves to emphasize the constitutional relationship between the State and the Crown when legislation that the Government intends to put before Parliament is outlined in a speech the sovereign delivers from the throne in the House of Lords. (Since Charles I attempted to arrest five members, the sovereign may not officially enter the House of Commons.)

The City's influence in national affairs is acknowledged every November when the prime minister attends the Lord Mayor's Banquet at Guildhall and accounts for government policies in a 'state of the nation' address. Heads of State on official visits to the sovereign are given a state banquet in the Great Hall; and members of the royal

family on special occasions or anniversaries (a coronation, silver jubilee, significant birthday) are honoured by the Corporation of the City of London with a luncheon at Guildhall.

At Guildhall, the centre of the City's government for eight hundred years, the Church has held little sway since the Reformation. The guilds, or livery companies as they are called today, the foundations of which had been based on semi-religious principles, became secular bodies. Refuges for the sick, the old and the poor, the hostels run by the monasteries for travellers and the learned societies that met in the cloisters were all swept away in the middle of the sixteenth century.

The City's administrative system is rooted in the ancient Court of Hustings where commercial disputes were resolved. It probably dated back to Saxon times and was succeeded by an elected Court of Common Council in the fourteenth century. The Court still sits once a fortnight to administer the City's estates and finances, to make decisions about its schools and arts organizations (the Guildhall School of Music and Drama, the Barbican Centre, the Museum of London), to hear reports on the open spaces it owns (Epping Forest, 500 acres in Surrey and Burnham Beeches) and to discuss its policies on domestic affairs and public services.

Guildhall's government was, in a small respect, the model for Parliament, but its democratic process does not extend to the election of the Lord Mayor. He (there has only been one woman) is selected from the Court of Aldermen by liverymen of the medieval craft guilds. The alderman chosen will have been a sheriff and is one of twenty-four heads of City wards, all of whom may remain members of the Court until the retirement age of seventy.

Within the City, only the sovereign takes precedence over the Lord Mayor who, since the reign of Elizabeth I, greets the monarch at Temple Bar on state occasions and demonstrates the City's loyalty by offering his Sword of State. This is returned and carried in front of the royal procession to signify that the sovereign is under his protection. The Lord Mayor also has a constitutional right to ask for an audience with the sovereign.

One of the ways the City acknowledges the Church is when the Dean of St Paul's imparts a blessing during the annual Lord Mayor's Show.

The incoming Lord Mayor, on his way to swear allegiance to the sovereign at the Royal Courts of Justice, alights from his carriage and goes into the south transept for the short service. After the Reformation, when any 'superstitious practices' engaged in by the livery companies were frowned upon, the guilds confined themselves to the commercial side of their work but gradually they have come round to acknowledging their religious obligations. Today, they have honorary chaplains; Court meetings are held on the feast day of the patron saint of the company; and their charitable work extends to financing old people's homes, maintaining the fabric of London's churches, subsidizing religious charities and administering schools. The Merchant Taylors', for example, governs the school of that name and the board of St Paul's School includes appointees of the Mercers' Company.

Great royal ceremonies of a religious kind are usually held at Westminster Abbey, though there are exceptions, as when the Prince of Wales chose St Paul's for his wedding to Lady Diana Spencer, just as Henry VII's eldest son had done almost five hundred years earlier. National ceremonies or occasions honouring prominent statesmen are more likely to be at St Paul's Cathedral, but there is no hard-and-fast rule. Elizabeth I went to old St Paul's for the Service of Thanksgiving after the Armada. State funerals for Nelson and Wellington were held at St Paul's, where they were buried, but Marlborough's was at Westminster Abbey. Centuries later, the funeral of Marlborough's descendant, Sir Winston Churchill, took place at St Paul's, but he was buried near Blenheim. Nor does any rule apply to secular state ceremonies. Addresses by important foreign Heads of State have been delivered in Westminster Hall, at Guildhall and in the Royal Gallery of the House of Lords.

However intricate the relationship between Church and State may be in practice, to an outsider they present a united front. The State looks impressive in London: the Houses of Parliament are its finest buildings. But the Church has a dominant position too: the monumental grandeur of St Paul's Cathedral, the splendours of Westminster Abbey but, most of all, the dozens of smaller churches—twenty-six by Christopher Wren—remind us through their strong visible presence that it is still important.

RIGHT: *A small, plain tablet in the crypt of St Paul's Cathedral is inscribed with a brief epitaph:* Lector, si monumentum requiris, Circumspice *(Reader, if you seek a memorial, look around you). It was placed on the grave of Sir Christopher Wren (1632–1723) by his son. Sir Christopher gave London its finest buildings: St Paul's is his masterpiece. The earlier, Gothic cathedral was ravaged by the Great Fire and pulled down; and Wren, his plans approved by Charles II, began work in 1675. Thirty-three years later, Wren, although in his seventies, was regularly hauled up to the lantern in a basket to supervise its completion. Only St Peter's in Rome, which took 120 years to build, can be compared to this monumental achievement by a single architect whose design was realized in only half a lifetime. Until the recent arrival of tower blocks, St Paul's majestically crowned London's skyline, the great dome complemented by the graceful, soaring spires on Wren's smaller churches.*

CHAPTER 3

Royal London

LONDON HAS BEEN HOME TO England's sovereigns for a thousand years, and most wished to build a great new palace in the capital. Not since the Tudor king, Henry VIII, has a monarch succeeded in doing so, though George IV achieved a compromise by conspiring with John Nash to rebuild Buckingham House.

Capital cities like Paris or Vienna, where no monarch reigns today, have large palaces that proclaim the might of a vanquished dynasty. London's many surviving 'royal' residences are more modest. While not as large or as grand as their Continental counterparts, they have a special allure; and all retain strong royal connections, even if some are not now occupied by the royal family.

Many of the palaces acquired by sovereigns still stand, not all in Westminster but often along the Thames between Greenwich and Hampton. Some, such as Hampton Court, Kensington Palace and Buckingham Palace, are lived in. Others, such as the palaces at Westminster and Greenwich, have been rebuilt to fulfil other roles.

At Greenwich, the palace begun by Charles II as a replacement for the Tudor Palace of Placentia was turned into a naval hospital by William III; and rooms for learned societies and government offices went up on the site of Somerset House, once the riverside dower house of Anne of Denmark, Henrietta Maria and Catherine of Braganza. Fragments of the rambling Stuart Palace of Whitehall, and of medieval Richmond and Eltham are still clearly visible; and the little Dutch House, where George III's brood of children grew up, today sits amid the botanical specimens at Kew, its royal links sometimes forgotten. Nonesuch, Bridewell and Chelsea Manor House, all built by Henry VIII, have vanished; and Carlton House, an unpretentious residence before the Prince Regent lavished a fortune on it, was demolished.

BELOW: *Charles II was given this statue of himself by Grinling Gibbons (gilded originally but later bronzed) in 1676. It has stood at the Royal Hospital, Chelsea, since 1692. Charles, inspired by Les Invalides in Paris, founded the retreat for army veterans.*

LEFT: *'One of the sublime sights of English architecture', Greenwich's palatial buildings have, paradoxically, never been a sovereign's home. Charles II began the west wing but died before it was finished; William and Mary had it completed as a hospital for retired seamen. England's most distinguished architects—Inigo Jones, Webb, Wren, Hawksmoor and Vanbrugh—all worked here.*

LEFT: *London's oldest royal palace has rarely been the sovereign's home. Gundulph, Bishop of Rochester, was instructed by William the Conqueror to build the Tower of London in 1078. Pale-coloured limestone brought from Normandy was used, but the White Tower only got its name after Henry III had drainpipes installed to stop discolouration by rainwater. William I's royal apartments, and the surviving Chapel of St John, were on the upper floor; the Constable of the Tower and the garrison were below. Henry III (1216–72), the only king to prefer the stronghold to Westminster, transformed the accommodation. He embellished existing buildings and added new private quarters, but all that remains is one chamber in the Wakefield Tower. His son, Edward I, turned the Tower into a massive fortress and put in a new water gate, later known as the notorious Traitors' Gate. The old river-gatehouse was strengthened and here, in what is called the Bloody Tower, the murder of the little princes by Richard III—a popular, but probably untrue, story—is said to have taken place.*

Only three royal buildings actually constructed for kings remain: the White Tower at the Tower of London; the little hunting lodge built by Henry VIII that became St James's Palace; and Clarence House, the cream stuccoed mansion designed by John Nash for William IV before he came to the throne.

The Tower of London is the oldest palace. One of three fortresses put up in the City to protect the Normans from 'the fickleness of the vast and fierce populace', it was built on William the Conqueror's orders in 1078 and is the only one to survive. Baynard's Castle stood near Blackfriars until the Great Fire, but nearby Montfichet had disappeared late in the thirteenth century.

Londoners considered the Tower a symbol of foreign authority (the chronicler William Fitz-Stephen said they believed the walls were cemented with the blood of wild animals to make it more ferocious). Henry II, who enlarged its defences, made it his headquarters during his long conflict with the barons and Simon de Montfort, and the pious Henry III had richly furnished royal apartments. Its reputation as a notorious prison partly deterred later sovereigns from living there: a fire at Westminster was the main reason Henry VIII was forced to occupy it for a period. Years later, after his secret marriage to Anne Boleyn, he had the royal apartments renovated for the festivities preceding her coronation. Ironically, Anne returned to face trial and execution at the Tower, a fate that also befell Catherine Howard, the only other wife of Henry's to spend the traditional night before a coronation at the Tower.

Until Henry VIII abandoned the Palace of Westminster after its partial destruction by fire in 1512, it had been home to twenty-two kings, from Canute to Henry VIII. Although it has long since become the Houses of Parliament, it still retains its royal status and comes under the control of the Lord Great Chamberlain. A further fire in 1834 destroyed almost all that remained of the medieval Palace. The Great Hall, begun by the Conqueror's son William Rufus in 1097, and the crypt were saved and incorporated into the decorative Victorian Gothic building designed by Sir Charles Barry and Augustus W. N. Pugin. The moated Jewel Tower, built in 1365, was far enough away to escape the fires and is now a museum.

RIGHT: *Henry VIII, England's most colourful sovereign, was born in the royal palace at Greenwich in 1491. In fifty-six years he had more homes than any other king. Three—St James's Palace, Hampton Court Palace and Windsor Castle—are still in use. His only memorial in London is this statue in a niche above the gateway of the city's oldest charitable institution, St Bartholomew's Hospital. In view of the role he played in the Reformation, this religious site may seem odd. But although the adjacent Augustinian priory was dissolved, the hospital managed to struggle on, and in 1546, at the request of Sir Richard Gresham, a wealthy City merchant, it was refounded and endowed by the King. The stone statue, commissioned in 1702, is thought to be the work of the sculptor Francis Bird.*

RIGHT: *Richard I (1157–99), a man considered the epitome of chivalry, is romantically nicknamed Coeur de Lion. He went to the Third Crusade and on his way home was captured and held to ransom. The Jews, however, do not have a high opinion of the King. In 1189, they were banished from his coronation banquet in the Palace of Westminster and then massacred. Richard spent only about a year of his life in England and could not speak the language. His second and last visit to his English kingdom was in 1194. He died of wounds received attacking the Castle of Chalus at Aquitaine. This fine Victorian equestrian statue of the eldest surviving son of Henry II and Eleanor of Aquitaine is by the Italian-born Royal Academician, Baron Carlo Marochetti. It stands outside the present Palace of Westminster. On the plinth, a bas-relief shows the Crusaders attacking the gates of Jerusalem.*

The Tudor gateway and basic structure of St James's Palace were built c.1535 when Henry VIII was still married to Anne Boleyn (their initials are carved into a fireplace in the tapestry room). When William III needed court apartments near Westminster, Sir Christopher Wren enlarged the hunting lodge, William Kent decorated part of it, and the little palace became the official home of the later Stuart and Hanoverian sovereigns. A fire in 1809 caused much destruction but some years later, during the period he was turning Buckingham House into a suitable residence for George IV, John Nash restored the fine State Apartments. The Tudor Chapel Royal—renovated in the 1830s—has been the scene of many royal weddings. When the present Prince of Wales, whose office is at the palace, succeeds to the throne, his accession—as are those of all sovereigns—will be proclaimed at St James's.

When Henry VIII left Westminster he owned several palaces and he quickly acquired more. At his accession in 1509, he had inherited Richmond, Eltham and Greenwich as well as the Norman fortresses at the Tower, Baynard's Castle and Windsor. In the country palace at Eltham, where Erasmus had met Henry VII's children, great Christmas feasts had been held in his father's reign but, in the early years of his marriage to Catherine of Aragon, these were transferred to Greenwich as Henry preferred the riverside pleasures of Placentia. He had been born at Greenwich and celebrated two of his marriages there—to Catherine of Aragon and Anne of Cleves.

Soon he had more palaces than wives. Not long after his move to the Tower, work began on a new palace close to the shrine of St Bride at the confluence of the Fleet and the Thames. At Bridewell, negotiations for his divorce from Catherine of Aragon were started and there, in 1529, he probably saw her for the last time. At Nonesuch, near Cheam, he put up a Renaissance extravaganza elaborately ornamented with gilded slate and stone; and the manor house he built at Chelsea he gave as a marriage gift to Katherine Parr. Richmond, where his father Henry VII had died and where Catherine of Aragon had given birth to two sons who died in infancy, was granted to Anne of Cleves in her divorce settlement. Cardinal Wolsey's fall from grace brought him Hampton Court and York House at Whitehall. The former he turned into one of the most luxurious palaces in the land. Jane Seymour came there for the birth of their son Edward VI (she died two weeks later), and his marriage ceremonies to the unfortunate Catherine Howard and to Katherine Parr were also held at Hampton Court.

Wolsey's London home was renamed the Palace of Whitehall and, until it burnt down, was the sovereign's principal residence. Additional land to the west was acquired for a bowling alley and tiltyard, and the parkland was enclosed for hunting. The medieval leper hospital dedicated to St James the Less was razed and replaced by the royal lodge that became St James's Palace. This palace is where the Court has been based since 1698: to this day ambassadors are accredited to the Court of St James. The Lord Chamberlain, who runs the royal household, has his offices there and the Duke and Duchess of Kent live in the wing known as York House.

LEFT: *The Queen's House at Greenwich was intended as a pleasure pavilion for Anne of Denmark whose husband, James I, had given her the adjacent Palace of Placentia in 1614. She died before Inigo Jones could finish it and the little Palladian villa was completed for Charles I's queen. But the Civil War intervened and the Tudors' favourite palace disappeared. After the Restoration, the widowed Henrietta Maria returned from exile and spent some time in her 'House of Delights'. She is the only queen known to have lived, albeit briefly, in the perfectly proportioned 'White House'.*

James I initiated a scheme to rebuild the sprawling Palace of Whitehall which ran in 'a heap of houses' for almost half a mile along the river, its 2,000 rooms accommodating the king, the royal family, ministers, courtiers and, in Charles II's reign, apartments for his mistresses. But of Inigo Jones's great plan only the Banqueting House was built. Any hopes that the beautifully proportioned classical palace Jones and John Webb designed for Charles I would be built waned when the Civil War intervened. Charles II asked Webb for a revised, less ambitious palace, and Wren also produced ideas. But the King's attention was focused on Greenwich and Windsor, and anyway he had it in mind to move the Court from London to Winchester where Wren actually started work on a palace to rival Versailles. Charles died before any designs were realized, and the Banqueting House was the only part of Whitehall to survive the fire of 1698. By then, William and Mary were on the throne and had moved to Kensington.

Less than a year after his arrival in England, William of Orange, a chronic asthmatic affected by the fog and damp river air at Whitehall, had bought the Earl of Nottingham's Jacobean house on higher ground at Kensington for £14,000. Sir Christopher Wren was instructed to improve it and also to make additions to the country palace at Hampton Court. The gardens immediately outside both palaces were laid out in formal patterns to resemble the Dutch garden at the royal palace of Het Loo in William's homeland.

Like her brother-in-law whom she detested, Queen Anne did not enjoy good health (besides her thirteen fruitless pregnancies, she was also arthritic), but she shared William's love for Kensington and for gardening. She built the Orangery ('a stately Green House') and used it as a 'Summer Supper House'. The State Apartments and King's Stairway were altered in George I's reign but George II, who made Kensington Palace his permanent home, made few changes, though he did indulge his wife's gardening schemes. Aided by Sir Robert Walpole, Queen Caroline let her husband believe she was paying for the landscaping. After her death, the King discovered she had raided the Treasury to transform a domestic retreat into a regal residence.

No sovereign has lived at Hampton Court or Kensington Palace since George II but the apartments in each have been 'grace and

BELOW: *James I and Charles I entertained at the magnificent Banqueting House Inigo Jones built at Whitehall in 1619–22. Torch-lit masques were forbidden c.1638 lest the ceiling paintings commissioned by Charles I from Rubens be damaged. The scaffold on which Charles was executed in January 1649 was erected outside the Banqueting House, the only substantial part of the Palace of Whitehall to survive.*

favour' homes assigned by the sovereign—at Hampton Court to people associated with the Court; at Kensington to members of the royal family. Today, the Prince and Princess of Wales, Princess Margaret and the families of two of the Queen's cousins live in separate quarters in Kensington. The State Apartments—not as well known as they deserve to be—are open to the public.

George III, whose parents had lived at Kew, enjoyed the country atmosphere and after the death of his mother, Augusta, Princess of Wales, in 1772, he spent the summer months at her former home, the White House. It was not a big house, certainly not large enough for the eight children he and Queen Charlotte by then had. The nearby Dutch House was acquired for the overflow, and in the grounds 'Farmer' George's children were given instructions on practical gardening and agriculture. Thirty years later, when the White House was demolished to make way for a huge, new, castellated palace which was never finished, the King and Queen moved to the Dutch House, or Kew Palace as the smallest royal residence in England was retitled.

LEFT: *Outside the State Apartments of Kensington Palace, the Carrara marble statue of Queen Victoria, sculpted by her daughter Louise in 1893, shows her at eighteen, her age when awakened on 20 June 1837 with the news of her uncle William IV's death. Thirty years later, Princess May of Teck (Queen Mary) was born in the same bedroom. Although five sovereigns— from William and Mary to George II—lived in the palace, neither queen returned to it after marrying. For almost 200 years the private apartments have housed close relatives of the monarch.*

LEFT: *The eldest of George III's large brood of children came to live with their tutors in tiny Kew Palace in 1773. When the youngest, Princess Amelia, was nineteen, the King and Queen also took up residence here. Four months before her death in November 1818, the Prince Regent wheeled his ailing mother, Queen Charlotte, into her drawing room to witness the marriages of her sons, the Duke of Clarence (William IV) and Edward, Duke of Kent (father of Queen Victoria). Their alliances had been hastily arranged to secure succession to the throne, after the death of the Prince Regent's daughter, Charlotte.*

George III used St James's for official functions when he came to town, while he and his family lived in Buckingham House. Considered the finest town house in London, it had been bought for £28,000 from Sir Charles Sheffield, the natural son of the Duke of Buckingham, as a replacement for Somerset House, the dower house of the Stuart queens. He and Queen Charlotte, whom he married in August 1761, liked it so much they made it their London home and took up residence there the following May. Most of their fifteen children were born in what was sometimes called the Queen's House after it was settled on Charlotte by Act of Parliament, but Buckingham House had to wait some considerable time before it was called a palace.

When the Prince of Wales came of age, George III gave Carlton House, his mother's home at the east end of The Mall, to his eldest son on the understanding that he was responsible for 'all repairs, taxes and the keeping of the garden'. The future Prince Regent paid little attention to his father's admonitions. He spent thirty years and a vast fortune turning his grandmother's modest house into the most expensively furnished and lavishly decorated palace in London. 'Overdone with finery', in the opinion of the architect Robert Smirke, it had a Corinthian portico (the columns now grace the National Gallery), a Chinese drawing room for which agents were sent to China for furniture, and sumptuous reception rooms for balls and assemblies.

By 1820, when George IV came to the throne, Carlton House was unsafe: its upper rooms were propped up for large presentations and some of it was shabby. Various architects came forward with schemes for a new palace but the King was not enthusiastic. A meddlesome Irish MP, Colonel Sir Frederick Trench, declaring he knew 'fifty noblemen much better lodged than their Sovereign', appointed himself 'an advocate for the *splendour* and magnificence of the crown' and invited Benjamin and Philip Wyatt to draw up plans for an enormous palace in Hyde Park with a two-mile triumphal route leading straight to St Paul's Cathedral. As several churches, Covent Garden and a chunk of Mayfair would have to be sliced through, even the Colonel was forced to admit it was 'the vision of a splendid impossibility'. The architect responsible for royal buildings, Sir John Soane, submitted a design for a massive palace set round three sides of a forecourt; and John Nash, who years

ABOVE: *An armada sails down The Mall: each cast-iron lamp post is surmounted by a galleon, to act as a reminder of Britain's naval supremacy.*

RIGHT: *A golden, winged figure of Victory, high above the seated figure of Queen Victoria, is one of many figures on the memorial to the Queen-Empress. A symbolic mother with three children faces Buckingham Palace; Truth and Justice are on the sides of the pillar with Courage and Constancy above them; and other allegorical figures, plus lions, a mermaid and a merman, are on the base or between the fountains. The memorial, which cost £325,000 and is made of marble, was unveiled in 1911 but not finished until after the First World War.*

RIGHT: *Buckingham Palace was Queen Victoria's home, but after Prince Albert's death in 1861 she rarely came to London. Bertie, her eldest son called it 'the Mausoleum', and when he came to the throne as Edward VII, extensive renovations were made to the State Rooms for the lavish receptions he and Queen Alexandra gave. Queen Mary later removed the heavy furnishings favoured by her in-laws. She rearranged rooms and rehung pictures, remarking on one occasion that 'it was not an easy task when one has miles of corridors to cover to find anything.' Most of the 600 rooms are now used either as reception rooms or as offices and domestic quarters for the royal household.*

earlier had had imaginative plans to transform Carlton House, also favoured a new palace. None appeared to please George IV who told Nash, 'I am too old to build a palace. If the public wish to have a palace, I have no objection to build one, but I must have a *pied-à-terre* ... and ... I will have it at Buckingham House. There are early associations which endear me to the spot.'

With Nash as an unwilling ally, the King embarked on an orgy of rebuilding his childhood home, his ideas getting more elaborate as work progressed. Parliament had been persuaded to finance the town house Nash proposed, but the King, delighting in handsome new State Rooms, declared, 'I think I shall hold my Courts there.' He had decided Buckingham House 'will make me an excellent palace'. Carlton House was pulled down, but not before the furniture and the priceless art treasures were trundled up The Mall and the mantlepieces and fixtures refitted in the formal apartments. The cost proved so enormous that Nash was hauled before two Parliamentary commissions to account for the overspending. He was dismissed and neither he nor George IV lived to see it finished. Edward Blore was called in to prepare it for William IV. Work was completed on 20 June 1837, four days before

the King died, and Victoria became the first sovereign to live at Buckingham Palace when she drove in state from Kensington to take up residence three weeks later.

During his long years in waiting as the Prince of Wales, Edward VII lived at Marlborough House, the large redbrick mansion Wren had built on Crown land for Sarah Churchill, Duchess of Marlborough. It reverted to royal ownership during the Regency and was renovated for Princess Charlotte, the Prince Regent's daughter, whose husband Leopold continued to live there after her death in childbirth in 1817. Leopold, later the first King of the Belgians, was the first widowed royal occupant. Queen Adelaide, Queen Alexandra and Queen Mary each came to Marlborough House on the death of their husbands.

At the time Nash was redesigning Buckingham House, the King's brothers decided they too needed palatial homes; they were, after all, in line of succession. Frederick, Duke of York, had owned a house in Stable Yard in St James's since 1806, but it wasn't until Princess Charlotte's death, when he became heir, that he called for major alterations to it. Something with larger proportions was called for. Benjamin Wyatt was still at work on York House when the Duke died owing huge sums of money. The government bought out the mortgages and sold the lease (the proceeds were used to buy Victoria Park in East London). Today, its name changed to Lancaster House, the 'grand old' Duke of York's house is used for government receptions.

Frederick's death made his brother William heir presumptive. As Ranger of Bushy Park, the Duke of Clarence had a country home close to Hampton Court and, in London, modest lodgings across Stable Yard which a reluctant John Nash was called upon to reconstruct. Clarence House, since refaced, was squeezed in by the side of St James's Palace and William IV and Queen Adelaide lived out their reign there. Buckingham House had been in the hands of the builders when George IV died in 1830, and remained so for a further seven years, while St James's Palace was too cramped for the royal household. An easy solution to this lack of space was effected: the small Tudor palace and Clarence House were joined by a passageway.

In the years since 1837, Clarence House has been the home of George III's daughter Augusta, of Queen Victoria's mother, the

ABOVE: *The reliefs on the Albert*
Memorial were carved in situ by
H. H. Armstead and J. B. Philip
who included only one living person
—Scott, its designer. These two
sixteenth and seventeenth-century
architects are Andrea Palladio
(with the dividers) and Giacomo
Barozzi da Vignola. Armstead
sculpted the poets, musicians and
painters; Philip the architects. They
were each paid £7,781. 15s. 0d. but
were later given a further £1,000 to
cover costs. By 1875, three years
after completion of the work, the
reliefs had become stained: the
suggestion that they be covered with
glass to preserve them has never
been adopted.

RIGHT: *Lancaster House was built alongside St James's Palace for George IV's brother, Frederick, Duke of York. The design, by Benjamin Wyatt, and its size, were largely influenced by the grandiose ideas of the Duke's amoureuse, Elizabeth, Duchess of Rutland. The Duke died in 1827 and the lease was sold to one of his creditors, the Marquess of Stafford, (later first Duke of Sutherland). Harriet, the wife of the second Duke was a great friend of Queen Victoria, a frequent visitor. The Queen greatly admired the state rooms and the famous Sutherland collection of Old Masters. She once announced her arrival by saying, 'I have come from my house to your palace.'*

RIGHT: *The Mall, the grand approach to Buckingham Palace, was made into what Queen Mary termed 'a fine wide carriage road going straight to the entry gate of the palace.' Early this century, it was lined with a double row of plane trees which on state occasions are interspersed with white flag poles, each one topped with a crown. The Union Jack flies on each if it is purely a British pageant, but for State Visits flags of the foreign Head of State fly from alternate poles. The Mall was not always a royal processional route. In Charles II's day, it was an unpretentious alley in St James's Park on which 'palle maille', a form of croquet, was played.*

Duchess of Kent, and her sons, Alfred, Duke of Edinburgh, and Arthur, Duke of Connaught. The Duke of Connaught died in 1942 and, after the war, the house was restored for Princess Elizabeth and the Duke of Edinburgh. On the death of George VI in 1952, they moved to Buckingham Palace, and Clarence House became the London home of Queen Elizabeth the Queen Mother.

'Buck House', as Londoners affectionately call it, has undergone many changes since its commanding presence in the park caused Queen Anne to say that the house built for John Sheffield, the first Duke of Buckingham, gave the appearance of owning all it surveyed. Nash and George IV gave its entrance a triumphal arch but this was banished to Marble Arch in 1850 when Blore, called back by Queen Victoria, hid Nash's country-style palace of Bath stone behind an east wing. This, in turn, was given a face-lift by Sir Aston Webb for George V and Queen Mary who thought a palace should look more impressive. A balcony and classical features were added to the plain façade and, as a memorial to Queen Victoria, The Mall was widened to make a grand processional way from Admiralty Arch to Buckingham Palace.

CHAPTER 4

Private Houses & Public Buildings

I T IS NOT ALWAYS EASY TO determine what goes on behind the windows of many buildings in the centre of London. In the last 150 years, social changes have altered the pattern of life and thousands of older houses in the City and the West End have undergone transformations. Once again, compromises have been necessary: palatial mansions were divided into flats; large town houses converted to company headquarters; family homes to offices; and a former terraced dwelling may well be a museum today. Private residences that once lined streets and squares are no longer lived in.

This situation started slowly, raced ahead in Victorian days and got its second wind more recently. Almost no new housing, except that at the Barbican, has been built in the City since the Second World War; and in Westminster the only significant additions this century have been the huge development at Dolphin Square in the late thirties and postwar blocks of apartments. Today, only the wealthy can afford the private houses and flats in Mayfair, St James's, Regent's Park and Knightsbridge. Embassies occupy many of Thomas Cubitt's stuccoed mansions in Belgravia and the substantial but more modest houses he built in Pimlico have been taken over by small hotels or converted into flats. Housing for the less well-off tends to be in blocks built by the council or charitable bodies such as the Peabody Trust. The best town houses close to the heart of London are in Kensington, Chelsea, Marylebone and Islington, while more modest terraced houses lie in the workaday boroughs of Southwark, Lambeth and Camden.

The growth of London as one of the world's great financial and commercial centres has meant that its people—now almost seven million—have spread into the liberties (the districts immediately beyond the City's jurisdiction) and the green fields of Essex, Kent,

BELOW: *The crowning glory of Regent's Park is Cumberland Terrace. The enormous pediment, the work of the little-known George Bubb, is filled with sculpture representing Britannia with 'the various arts, sciences, trades, etc., that mark her empire'.*

LEFT: *Built in 1827 and named after George IV's brother, Ernest, Duke of Cumberland, the terrace has the appearance of a grand palace and John Nash's first plans show it facing a* guinguette *for the Prince Regent. In revised drawings, the villa has disappeared. The scale of the terrace is impressive, and deceptive: dozens of private residences have been created out of once much larger houses. James Elmes, who published* Metropolitan Improvements *in 1827, did not approve of the squat vases. His opinion was that 'Lord Byron scarcely hated a dumpy woman more than I hate these dumpy jars of the apothecary.'*

Middlesex and Surrey. The loss of residents in the city centre is due not only to the demand for business premises and the availability of modern transport to and from the suburbs, but also to the fact that most property was leasehold and reverted to developers able to finance subsequent rebuilding. It must also be remembered that until after the Second World War the majority of householders did not own their own homes, especially in central areas where there were complicated rental agreements with freeholders. The single-family house with a plot of garden has been a dream realized in suburbia at the cost of the closely-knit communities of the two-up, two-down terraced houses that were the essence of family life in the city.

Since London has become a commercial metropolis into which people commute every day, the character of 'the capital of capitals' has completely altered. Napoleon's reference to England being a nation of shopkeepers was not quite the deprecating remark some imagine. The comment, gleaned from a book Bonaparte had read, was a perceptive observation on the way Londoners had lived and worked since medieval times. The private house and market place were invariably one and the same, and even the revolution of trade in the Elizabethan era brought about only gradual change. Professional men saw their clients in ground-floor chambers in their homes; merchants did the same, or met in coffee houses to discuss their affairs; tradesmen and craftsmen sold goods on the lower floors of houses, and at the end of the day the shop owner retired upstairs, leaving the assistants to sleep underneath the counters.

It is a way of life that has now virtually died away, although earlier this century it was not unusual to find bank managers occupying houses beside or above the bank, shopkeepers living over their shops and doctors with surgeries in their homes. An exception is the Inns of Court where many barristers still have flats in the same buildings as their chambers.

The expansion of trade in the sixteenth and seventeenth centuries saw the beginning of the separation of shop and dwelling. London overtook Antwerp as the most important commercial city in the world soon after Sir Thomas Gresham built the Royal Exchange. Realizing that England's deteriorating relationship with Spain was causing

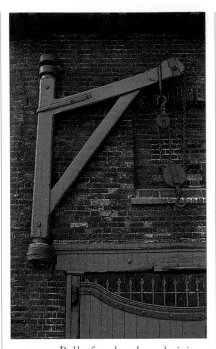

ABOVE: *Bells for church and civic buildings all over the world have been cast at the Bell Foundry in Whitechapel Road. For many years the raw materials were hauled up on this winch. Twenty-three years after Robert Mot established his business in 1570, he recast one of Westminster Abbey's bells; since then the remaining seven bells have been made by this firm. Big Ben, the Liberty Bell and the Bicentennial Bell, presented by Queen Elizabeth II to the people of the United States of America in 1976, all came from Whitechapel.*

CHURCH BELL FOUNDRY

ESTABLISHED
A.D. 1570

BELL FOUN DRY

BELL FOUN DRY

LEFT: *The present Whitechapel Road premises, occupied continuously since 1738 by the Church Bell Foundry, are the most remarkable early industrial buildings left in London. There is some evidence that the company, the oldest in the capital, was trading in Houndsditch for a century before Robert Mot moved outside the City walls. It is one of the few places where the pattern of life in former centuries may be appreciated. Orders and records would have been maintained in the shop, while the family probably lived upstairs, or in one of the adjoining houses where staff and foundry workers would have had sleeping quarters.*

LEFT: *Gray's Inn is one of four Inns of Court; lawyers qualified to practise at the English bar have lived and worked here since it was established in the fifteenth century on land owned by the de Gray family in Holborn. The historic Great Hall, in which Shakespeare's* The Comedy of Errors *was first staged in 1594, the chapel, and the library with its valuable collection of books, were destroyed by enemy action in May 1941. Fortunately, such features as the carved screen in the hall and stained-glass windows had been removed for safe-keeping and were replaced in the restored buildings. In the gardens, 'The Walks' are said to have been laid out by Sir Francis Bacon, one of several great Elizabethan members of the Inn.*

LEFT: *Each Inn of Court is an Honorable Society administered by Benchers who call students to the bar. The records of Lincoln's Inn go back to 1292, though the present site near Chancery Lane has only been occupied by the society since the beginning of the fifteenth century. The library, which has the country's most important collection of legal books, was begun in 1492. The chapel, often ascribed to Inigo Jones but probably by John Clarke, rests on vaulted arcades where students still 'walk and talk and confer for their learnings'. The poet John Donne, a member of the Inn, was Dean of St Paul's when he laid the chapel's foundation stone and later preached the sermon at the service of consecration in 1623.*

trading difficulties, he was persuaded to give London a bourse, or 'a place for merchants to assemble'. It was built at Gresham's expense on land purchased by 750 citizens and opened in 1570 by Elizabeth I who, John Stow records, viewed 'every part ... especially the pawn, which was richly furnished with all sorts of the finest wares in the city.' The building, on the site of the third and present Victorian exchange, was set around a courtyard. In booths on the colonnaded walks, merchants transacted their business, and on the first floor there were the shops (Stow's 'pawn') of milliners, booksellers and goldsmiths. A direct result of business generated at the new exchange was the establishment of the great trading companies, among them the East India Company and the Hudson Bay Company which survives today.

Before the founding of the Royal Exchange, unless a craftsman or trader belonged to an ancient guild, there were few large places for people to meet and it was almost unheard of for a professional or businessman to repair to a separate office building. Liverymen (so

RIGHT: *The Jamaica Wine House is on the site of Pasqua Rosee's, London's first coffee house. An advertisement, thought to have been issued sometime between 1652 and 1656, informs customers that coffee is 'made and sold in St Michael's Alley in Cornhill by Pasqua Rosee at the Signe of his own Head.'*
After the Great Fire it became known as the Jamaica Coffee House because the merchants who congregated there imported goods from the West Indies. When coffee houses ceased to be rendezvous where traders met, the Jamaica stayed in business by converting to a wine merchant's. In 1869, the present terracotta tavern was built.

RIGHT: *The Apothecaries' Society is one of the younger City livery companies. Its charter was only granted in 1617 when it broke away from the Grocers', but it boasts one of the oldest halls. The society bought Lady Howard of Effingham's house in 1634 but this, and forty-three older livery halls, was wiped out in the Great Fire. The present hall was erected in 1688, though the façade in Blackfriars Lane (right) is an eighteenth-century addition. Students wishing to dispense medical remedies studied with the society. A young man who came from Ireland intending to be a chemist worked at the new physic garden which the society was creating in Chelsea on land it had originally leased to accommodate its ceremonial barge. Hans Sloane, the royal physician, later repaid the society for the start it had given to his brilliant career.*

LEFT: *The Royal Hospital, Chelsea, was begun by Charles II, whose inspiration was Les Invalides in Paris. Romantic legend insists it was Nell Gwynne's idea (a plaque in the Great Hall acknowledges her interest), but the Paymaster-General Sir Stephen Fox had previously outlined the plan to the King. In May 1682, John Evelyn went with Fox and Sir Christopher Wren to show the 'designe of the College to be built at Chelsey for emerited Souldiers' to the Archbishop of Canterbury. Evelyn said it would accommodate '440 Persons with Governor and Officers'. The hospital, described by Carlyle as 'quiet and dignified . . . the work of a gentleman', is still run on military lines: a governor and officers are in charge of six companies of in-pensioners whose distinctive red uniforms date from the first Duke of Marlborough's time.*

LEFT: *Until the Reformation, hospitals were run by religious orders; thereafter, most were taken over and maintained by the City livery companies or endowed by rich merchants. By the eighteenth century, the hospitals could not cope with the enlarged population and growth of disease in slum areas. As a result of a charitable organisation set up to assist the 'Sick Poor and Needy', a number of hospitals were established whose income came from voluntary subscriptions. Guy's Hospital in Southwark, founded in 1722 by Thomas Guy, was one of the first such hospitals, and the original buildings are set around two courtyards. Sitting on the lawn in the inner quadrangle is a stone alcove. This had been added to old London Bridge in 1752 and was brought to its present site when the bridge was rebuilt early in the nineteenth century.*

called because each company has its own livery or uniform) of the craft and merchant guilds met at their companies' halls to set guidelines about the quality and standards of workmanship and to fix prices. In some ways, they were the prototype of the modern trade union. Since a large number had been in existence long before the Poor Laws were passed or a social security system invented, they also undertook charitable and welfare work, and made elaborate arrangements for members' funerals. The halls were also a centre of a liveryman's social life—which they still are.

While the City companies have maintained their charitable associations and many have almshouses and educational responsibilities, the majority no longer represent their original crafts. But there are exceptions, and the Goldsmiths', the Fishmongers' and the Vintners' are still closely connected with their trades.

None of the splendidly decorated livery halls that survived the Great Fire remain, but many of the present-day halls are on the same sites they occupied in the fourteenth and fifteenth centuries; the Skinners' have been on Dowgate Hill since about 1380 and the Vintners' in

LEFT: *Staple Inn on Holborn is the only Tudor domestic building in central London. Thousands of similar gabled, half-timbered houses, with oriel windows and overhanging upper floors, once stood in the city's streets and lanes. They disappeared during the three September days that the Great Fire raged in 1666. Before it became a legal Inn of Chancery in the fifteenth century, it was a meeting place for wool-staplers. In a house (now gone) where he lived overlooking the quadrangle at the rear, Dr Johnson sat up writing every night for a week to earn sufficient money to pay for his mother's funeral. Staple Inn was unsympathetically restored after the Second World War.*

LEFT: *Because the Great Fire stopped at Cock Lane, Smithfield, buildings to the north of it were saved. These two redbrick houses in Cloth Fair, with protruding bay windows, are rare—if heavily restored—examples of early seventeenth-century residences. The name of the street comes from the cloth fair that was held here for centuries. Inigo Jones, the son of a draper, was probably born in Cloth Fair in 1573; he was baptized in the adjoining Church of St Bartholomew's in July of that year. Centuries later, the poet and architectural enthusiast Sir John Betjeman, who lived in the street for over twenty years, recalled that in his younger days a shop selling cloth had still existed. The courts and alleys by the side of the church have faint echoes of pre-Fire London.*

LEFT: *'Very tastefully disposed', was a Victorian writer's comment on Spencer House in St James's Place. This palatial house overlooking Green Park was designed by John Vardy and remodelled by James 'Athenian' Stuart. It was built in 1756–66 for John, the first Earl Spencer, who had secretly married his childhood sweetheart, Georgiana Poyntz, in 1755, on the day after he came of age. One room, dedicated to the theme of love and marriage, was decorated to honour Georgiana, an ancestor of Diana, Princess of Wales. The Spencer family, which has not lived in the house since the 1920s, has recently leased the house to Lord Rothschild who has restored the reception rooms to their original neo-classic splendour.*

LEFT: *The City of London has had a mayor for over 800 years, but the First Citizen did not have an official residence until the middle of the eighteenth century. Before 1752, when Sir Crisp Gascoyne moved into the Mansion House, the Lord Mayor entertained and received visitors at his livery hall. The house was designed by the City Surveyor, George Dance the Elder, who was influenced by Palladio's follower Colen Campbell. The imposing façade, with six Corinthian columns and a pediment sculpted by Robert Taylor, remains as Dance intended; two attic storeys have been removed, however (one by his son), and other alterations or additions have been made to the interior.*

Upper Thames Street since 1446. These two companies, like the Apothecaries' in Blackfriars Lane, have halls that were built in the decade after the Fire, though all have been heavily restored.

Less formal transactions were conducted at the beginning or end of the day in the hundreds of coffee houses that proliferated in London. Here, business and pleasure were combined when traders and merchants met to negotiate and sign contracts. From 1652, when Pasqua Rosee's opened in St Michael's Alley, Cornhill, the coffee house was the popular place to meet and confer.

Owners vied to attract and keep customers, supplying an assortment of services—the latest pamphlets, news sheets, domestic and foreign newspapers, bulletins, customs forms, auction notices and price lists. Bags for letters were hung up prominently and the owners had well-organized arrangements with ships' captains for these to be forwarded, a practice which the Post Office tried in vain to curb.

Quacks and imposters promoted cures for ailments and dispensed them at coffee houses. Thomas Smith of King Street, Westminster, the self-styled 'first Master Corn-cutter of England' advertised that he would visit twenty-one coffee houses daily 'to serve any Gentleman or Lady', though where exactly in the building and how he performed the pedicures is not recorded.

Many insurance schemes, such as the Fire Office in which the rascal Nicholas Barbon was a prime mover, began in coffee houses. Edward Lloyd, who opened in Tower Street in 1688, had an arrangement with the Post Office to have the latest shipping news to hand. Shipowners, merchants and sea captains involved in waterborne trades congregated there and Lloyd's got the reputation as the best place to obtain marine insurance. It remained a coffee house—in Lombard Street from 1692 —until 'a very roomy and convenient place' was rented in the Royal Exchange in 1774, and there Lloyd's stayed until 1928. The Royal Exchange lasted only a further eleven years; trading ceased in 1939.

At about the same time as Edward Lloyd moved to Lombard Street, Jonathan's Coffee House in Exchange Alley became the recognized place for 'Stock-Jobbing'. John Houghton, in his weekly journal *Husbandry & Trade*, described in 1694 how 'the Monied Man goes

RIGHT: *The Bank of England has been rebuilt several times since it came to Threadneedle Street in 1734, but only the windowless curtain wall of the admired late eighteenth-century building by Sir John Soane remains. Sir Herbert Baker's ten-storey replacement, erected in 1921–37, incorporated another, even earlier, feature— Robert Taylor's Court Room.*

RIGHT: *Somerset House is a fine example of Georgian classical architecture. When the royal house on the site fell into disrepair, Sir William Chambers, at the request of George III, built government offices and rooms for three learned societies—the Royal Academy of Arts, the Royal Society and the Society of Antiquaries. These bodies have all since moved, but in 1990 the Academy's former galleries in the Strand block were hung with paintings belonging to the Courtauld Institute of Art.*

RIGHT: *Cheyne Walk in Chelsea has some of the finest private houses in London; and No 5 had one of the strangest occupants, the well-known miser, John Camden Neild. On his death in 1852, he left his fortune of £500,000 to Queen Victoria who, after she had assured the future security of Neild's servants, spent the inheritance on her new Scottish home, Balmoral Castle. Artists and writers have always been attracted to the houses overlooking the river— George Eliot lived in No 4. A small tablet by the entrance to Cheyne Mews recalls that this is the site of Henry VIII's manor house; a mulberry tree there is said to have been planted by Elizabeth I when she was a girl.*

RIGHT: *No 16 Cheyne Walk is called the Queen's House because there are thought to be links with Catherine of Braganza; for no apparent reason, it is also known as the Tudor House. Like No 5, it has splendid wrought-iron gates and had an equally eccentric but rather more famous resident. Shortly after the death of his wife, Lizzie Siddal, in 1862, the pre-Raphaelite free spirit Dante Gabriel Rossetti came here to enjoy a fairly Bohemian lifestyle. At one time he shared the house with the poet Algernon Swinburne, and a menagerie. The constantly escaping wombat, armadillos and other animals led to a clause in the lease forbidding future tenants to keep wild animals.*

among the Brokers (which are chiefly upon the Exchange), and at Jonathan's Coffee House, sometimes at Garroway's and at some other Coffee Houses and asks how Stocks go and upon information bids the broker to buy or sell so many shares of such and such stocks.' Thirty years later, 150 dealers rented Jonathan's for their exclusive use but the tenancy was short-lived—a broker who had been denied access went to court and won—and it wasn't until 1773 that a building close to the Bank of England in Threadneedle Street was bought by a group of brokers and named the Stock Exchange. Anyone could rent space on the floor for 6d. a day.

Even the mighty Bank of England waited forty years before the decision was taken to have its own building across the street from the Royal Exchange. Originally the bank occupied Mercers' Hall, then moved to Grocers' Hall in Poultry and in 1734 George Sampson designed the first of its buildings in Threadneedle Street.

The Baltic Exchange, Lloyds, the Stock Exchange and many insurance companies that began trading in coffee houses or the Royal

RIGHT: *The College of Arms in Queen Victoria Street has been part of the royal household for 700 years. The officers—the Earl Marshal, the three Kings of Arms, heralds and pursuivants—examine family records and have the right to grant arms to eminent people. (They refused Shakespeare's father.) The Earl Marshal, a title held by the earls or dukes of Norfolk since the fourteenth century, arranges such great state occasions as coronations; his own throne is in the Court Room. The College has been based in the City since 1555, when it was given the town house of the earls of Derby. This was rebuilt after the Great Fire, and saved from another fire during the Second World War by a change of wind. The gates, which were sent for scrap metal, were replaced in 1956 by gilded wrought-iron gates and railings from a house in Herefordshire.*

RIGHT: *Horace Walpole considered that the heavy, early eighteenth-century portico of the Admiralty was 'deservedly veiled' by Robert Adam's graceful screen which has playful sea horses atop the pilasters. Thomas Ripley, a friend of Walpole's father, Sir Robert the Prime Minister, had replaced Christopher Wren's Admiralty building in Whitehall with a sombre, brick building. The interior has many fine rooms and carvings by Grinling Gibbons.*

Exchange are today in separate headquarters in the City. The transition that had started in the eighteenth century gained momentum in 1838 when a fire destroyed the Royal Exchange and brought to light the need for individual offices and exchanges. Its temporary loss speeded up the emigration of the City's population, which had risen from about 80,000 in 1550 to almost 150,000 in 1700. By 1841, when the Census recorded 123,000 residents, private dwellings still outnumbered offices, but forty years later the population had dropped to 51,000. In 1990 only 4,700 people lived in the City, most of them residents in the new homes in the brutal concrete towers, flats and maisonettes at the Barbican, or caretakers at large companies.

In order to accommodate the new business premises of the past century and a half, the last of the medieval houses, elegant Georgian crescents and rows of solid Victorian buildings have been decimated; and huge rebuilding since the Second World War has produced a brave-new-world wilderness of box constructions which pierce the skyline. These faceless, high-tech blocks have no decorative features to leaven their harsh straight lines, and only succeed in emphasizing the elegant classical pediments and columns of surviving period buildings such as Guildhall, the Bank of England, the Royal Exchange, the City churches and older livery halls. These older public buildings, the City's remaining examples of more gracious architecture, have a dignity that symbolizes the power of the great City institutions and trading companies. No mirror-glazed tower can compete with their distinguishing features, though their architects and occupants will argue that space-age technology requires post-modern architecture.

Finding the scattered evidence of dwellings built in the City before or immediately after the Great Fire is like looking for a jewel in a forest of stalagmites today. Two early examples have been re-erected elsewhere in London. The intricately carved façade of the house Sir Paul Pindar built in Bishopsgate in the 1620s is in the Victoria and Albert Museum; and fifteenth-century Crosby Hall, where later Richard III was told of the death of the little princes, has been on Chelsea Embankment since early this century. (Once owned by Sir Thomas More, it is now in his former garden.) Two restored Jacobean timber-framed plaster houses remain in Cloth Fair, and there are a few late seventeenth-century brick houses in the Temple and two from the reign of Queen Anne on Laurence Pountney Hill. The Mansion House, the elegant residence built in 1752 by George Dance the Elder for the Lord Mayor, is the only large house to have withstood the onslaught.

Fortunately, immediately outside the present City boundaries, the occasional Tudor house has survived, and in Spitalfields a hint of life in early eighteenth-century London has been preserved in Fournier Street where attics with wide windows were added to the tall brick houses to enable the Huguenot silk-weavers to take advantage of fading light. In surrounding Whitechapel, which Stow considered 'pestered with cottages and alleys', emigrants and the less well-off have lived cheek by

RIGHT: *Kenwood, the 'noble seat' of the earls of Mansfield on Hampstead Heath, was saved in 1925 when plans to build on the surrounding woodland were afoot. Edward Guinness, the first Earl of Iveagh, intervened and bought the estate. It was his wish that the house, by Robert Adam, be preserved as a fine example of an eighteenth-century gentleman's home. On his death two years later, Lord Iveagh left Kenwood and a remarkable collection of paintings to a trust. Robert Adam had completely remodelled another house for the first Earl of Mansfield in 1767; and the central structure and splendidly decorated rooms at Kenwood are largely Adam's work. His contemporary, Angelica Kauffmann, painted the ceiling in the hall and her husband, the Venetian artist Antonio Zucchi, was responsible for the murals in the 'Adam Room'.*

LEFT: *The hill-top village of Hampstead was a spa frequented by the carriage trade early in the eighteenth century. Chalybeate spring water was discovered in Well Walk and the wealthy and fashionable came to take a cure. The water was bottled and sold in flasks in a nearby street which became known as Flask Walk (left). With delightful streets and original Georgian houses, the village today lives up to its description as one of the 'Politest Public Places in England'. This observation was made before the long-vanished Assembly Room was forced to close because loose ladies and gamblers were giving the neighbourhood a bad name.*

LEFT: *Keats House in Hampstead was the home of the poet John Keats from 1818 until consumption forced him to winter in Italy two years later. On 23 February 1821, at the age of twenty-five, he died in Rome. In his day, the house was semi-detached and his fiancée, Fanny Brawne, lived next door with her widowed mother. A number of his great works—'La Belle Dame sans Merci', sonnets and 'Lamia'— were written in the house. Under a plum tree in the garden he wrote the famous 'Ode to a Nightingale'. The tree has been replaced but several other trees (still saplings in 1820) now shelter the garden. Personal ephemera, including Fanny's engagement ring, are displayed in the house.*

jowl in tightly-packed hovels for hundreds of years. The filthy conditions of Elizabethan times, deplored by the historian who thought it 'no small blemish to so famous a city to have so unsavoury and unseemly an entrance' on the main road to the City through Aldgate, were replaced by dingy tenements which are only gradually disappearing in the late twentieth century.

In the West End, where some thought was given to the way people lived when the streets and squares were planned, it is easier to identify the role of a building. Large numbers of eighteenth and nineteenth-century houses remain, their external appearance hardly betraying the internal conversions. On dark evenings, only strip neon lighting and an absence of curtains reveals that drawing rooms and bedrooms are now offices, though occasionally developers have left a small flat at the top of some buildings. Mews, where stables and horses gave way to garages and motorcars at the turn of this century, have become town houses. Detached mansions, such as Crewe House, are often no longer in

aristocratic hands; two stately homes in St James's, Spencer House and Bridgewater House, are luxurious offices, though the fine rooms in the former are used for private receptions and there is palatial living accommodation in Bridgewater House for the head of the overseas company which owns it. At Cambridge House in Piccadilly, a means of combining home comforts with limited public use was found when this former royal residence was turned into the Naval and Military Club; but two great Park Lane houses of noblemen were demolished in the late 1920s to make way for the Dorchester and Grosvenor House hotels. Other elegant homes of important men have been taken into state care. The Admiralty, the First Lord's house, originally had just one room for board meetings and, while it still has accommodation, many more rooms are now offices. Lord Melbourne's distinguished town house, with its huge Venetian window overlooking Horse Guards Parade, has become the Scottish Office; and Gwydyr House in Whitehall is today the Welsh Office.

Where a building has been designed for a special purpose and its use has not changed, the result is almost always appropriate and pleasing. The Natural History Museum has exuberant displays of animals and plants carved in the stonework; the classical façade of the National Gallery declares its importance; and the dignified entrance to the British Museum makes a statement about its rich collections of antiquities and art.

But the dichotomy between private houses and public buildings can be seen in an awkward trio of houses in Lincoln's Inn Fields where different façades give the impression of separate residences. Few clues reveal that they are in fact a fascinating museum. The houses were built beween 1792 and 1824 by the architect Sir John Soane who lived in one but connected the three to display what earlier collectors would have called a somewhat large 'cabinet of curiosities'. He left the paintings, antiquities and architectural drawings to the nation with instructions that his house and museum should be kept 'as nearly as possible in the state' they were in at the time of his death in 1837.

In the nineteenth century, as the Empire expanded, an increased demand for public buildings was necessitated by the United Kingdom's importance as a world power and London's fast-growing population (it multiplied four times to 4,500,000 between 1800 and 1900). The Victorians responded by organizing architectural competitions for the new Royal Exchange (won by Sir William Tite and built 1841–4) and for new government offices in Whitehall. The judges' decision for the Foreign Office and the Home Office was overruled by Lord Palmerston, the Prime Minister, who was about to select his own architect, when Sir George Gilbert Scott, whose designs had been the second choice of the architectural assessors, objected. He lobbied Parliament and won his case, though his attempts to 'Gothicize the whole country', as Palmerston claimed, were forestalled by the Prime Minister who insisted on the Italian style.

Further competitions were held for proposed museums on land acquired with the profits of the Great Exhibition that Prince Albert had organized in 1851. Eighty-seven acres in South Kensington had

ABOVE: *This lion is one of innumerable domestic, wild and sometimes extinct creatures that occupy every cranny on the Natural History Museum in South Kensington. The flora and fauna, and a profusion of gargoyles, were carved on to capitals, friezes, arches and towers, and represent different aspects of the great collections housed inside the museum.*

RIGHT: *Sir Alfred Waterhouse designed the Natural History Museum in a Romanesque style at a time when German cathedral architecture was popular in England. The exterior was banded in stripes of buff and blue terracotta. One of the first institutions in 'Museumland', this branch of the British Museum opened in 1881 when lack of space in Bloomsbury forced the museum to move its natural history and botanical collections. Many of the exhibits had come from Sir Hans Sloane's 'noble cabinet', the Royal Society's 'repository' and Sir Joseph Banks' huge botanical collection. The large halls with vaulted ceilings and great arcades contain dinosaurs, stuffed birds, butterflies and skeletons of men and beasts. Scientific laboratories and rooms for research studies occupy a considerable section of the building.*

RIGHT: *Before it became government offices late in the last century, the Scottish Office in Whitehall had had three aristocratic owners—Frederick, Duke of York, the first Viscount Melbourne and Lord Dover. In 1812, the house was at the centre of a great scandal. Melbourne's son, William Lamb (later the Victorian Prime Minister), his neurotic wife and their baby boy lived on the upper floors. Here, in the room behind the Venetian window overlooking Horse Guards Parade, began an affair which rocked society and has proved fascinating ever since. Lady Caroline Lamb was visited by the poet she had contrived to meet some days earlier. Her liaison with the 'mad, bad and dangerous to know' Lord Byron was the talk of the town, more because of Caroline's 'wild and imprudent' behaviour than Byron's reputation as an insatiable lover.*

RIGHT: *Albany, the residential chambers set at the back of a courtyard, was built by Sir William Chambers in 1770–4 for Lord Melbourne. Soon after, Melbourne exchanged this Piccadilly house for one in Whitehall owned by the Duke of York, whose second title was Albany. When the Duke left in 1802, the house was converted into apartments for bachelors. Lord Byron moved to 2A in the spring of 1814 and was at once invaded at all hours of the day by the frantic 'Caro' Lamb, who had discovered she was not the only woman in his life. 'The moment the door is open in she walks', he wrote to her sympathetic mother-in-law, adding that while he couldn't throw her out of the window, 'all bolts, bars and silence can do to keep her away are done daily and hourly'.*

LEFT: *When Lord Palmerston insisted that the Foreign and Commonwealth Office reflect Italy, Sir George Gilbert Scott 'bought himself some costly books on Italian architecture' to refresh his knowledge and to show he was 'not behind with the classicists'. The resulting building, dating from 1861, is covered in pilasters, Corinthian columns, statues, medallions, balconies and balustrades and a tower, all combining to look like an overdone Italian palazzo. India, the favourite jewel in Queen Victoria's Empire, had a separate office in the building. This was reached through the profusely adorned, glazed courtyard. The majolica friezes, statues and polished granite columns were part of a plan by Scott's contemporary, Sir Matthew Digby Wyatt.*

been bought by the Commissioners and a number of plans were put forward over a period of fifty years before the Natural History Museum, the Victoria and Albert Museum and the other educational, scientific, musical, artistic and technical institutions were completed in the district some Victorians called Albertopolis.

In the 1860s, the competition that sparked the imagination of architects was the plan to resite the Law Courts to the north of the Strand. Since the removal of the courts from Winchester to London in the thirteenth century and until the destruction of the Palace of Westminster in 1834, civil cases had been heard in Westminster Hall, except outside term time when they were forced to move to courts all over London. Eleven leading architects were invited to submit plans for what would be, after the Houses of Parliament, the most important new building in the country. The decision to concentrate the sprawling legal system in one area close to the Inns of Court resulted in G. E. Street's Gothic-style Royal Courts of Justice.

The prosperity founded on the Industrial Revolution and the Empire achieved a more prominent face in the vainglorious Victorian attempts to show off new wealth. Public buildings advertised the importance of an organization, and large private houses, such as 58 Knightsbridge (now the French Embassy), paraded the self-aggrandizement of their directors. This form of promotion reached its zenith during the age of railway mania, and no one announced his presence in the capital more loudly than George Hudson. Dubbed the 'Railway King' by Sydney Smith, Hudson controlled one-fifth of the country's network when he bought himself one of the largest houses in London at Albert Gate. In this Knightsbridge home, until he overreached himself financially and misappropriated shareholders' money, he and his wife entertained on a lavish scale, to the derisive amusement of cartoonists.

Like the companies the Yorkshire-born Hudson was associated with, most railways originated in the provinces and their owners were determined to make sure London knew they had arrived. Each terminus sought to display its importance by putting up a station and an hotel to publicize the destinations it served. At Victoria, where the words 'the Gateway to the Continent' were carved into the frieze, French and Italian architecture influenced the design of the Grosvenor

LEFT: *Many railway companies had their origins in the provinces, and their owners were determined to trumpet their importance when they arrived in London. The hotel at St Pancras, the terminus of the Midland Railway, was the most exuberant. A High Gothic mixture of pinnacles and gables with elaborate ironwork, it bears more resemblance to a German castle than a railway hotel. The legend that Sir George Gilbert Scott (1811–78) reused his rejected designs for the Foreign Office is totally false. He was a Gothic enthusiast 'glad to be able to erect one building in that style in London', though he prefaced his comment by saying, 'my own belief is that it is possibly too good for its purpose.' The hotel closed in 1935, since when it has been used as offices.*

LEFT: *A pillar emblazoned with the colourful insignia of the London Chatham and Dover Railway and massive cast-iron supports, looking curiously Egyptian in the Thames by Blackfriars Bridge, are the only memories of the attractive wrought-iron, lattice girder bridge that once brought passengers to Blackfriars Station from Europe and the suburbs. One of two railway crossings at this point, it was designed in the 1860s by Joseph Cubitt to complement his Blackfriars (road) Bridge. The Holborn Viaduct Company's less pleasing bridge has survived. Pilasters carved with the exotic and suburban destinations advertised by the LCDR—Florence, Leipsic [sic] and St Petersburg or Beckenham, Bromley and Ramsgate—were removed from outside the station in 1977. Today, stones of false promise, they are set into a wall by platform two.*

LEFT: *A blue plaque outside the Naval and Military Club at 94 Piccadilly announces that the 'In and Out'—so called because of the conspicuous markings on the gateposts—was once the home of Viscount Palmerston and a former royal residence. There is nothing to substantiate the stories that Queen Victoria, on a visit to her uncle Adolphus, Duke of Cambridge, was attacked by a madman in the courtyard, or that in 1863, when he was Prime Minister and nearly eighty, Lord Palmerston committed adultery here with a servant. The Naval and Military Club, founded in 1862, was the first club to move to Piccadilly, and has occupied the house since it acquired the lease shortly after Palmerston's death. The house itself was designed a century earlier by Matthew Brettingham for the Earl of Egremont.*

Hotel. The industries of the Midlands were promoted in the neo-Gothic hotel at St Pancras which was built entirely with materials brought from Coventry, Leicester, Nottingham and Rutland. Charing Cross's French Renaissance style hinted that Paris was not far away, though Athens can only have been a fantasy for those who went through the gateway to Birmingham at Euston. The £35,000 spent on the massive Greek arch designed by Philip Hardwick in 1838 was justified by the London and Birmingham Railway when it told its shareholders in a report that, as the entrance to the London passenger station would immediately open up 'the Grand Avenue for travelling between the Midlands and Northern parts of the Kingdom, the directors thought that it should receive some embellishment.' Outraged protests greeted the news that the Euston arch was to be demolished when the station was rebuilt in 1963–8, but down it came and the station, like most termini today, is awash with primary-coloured fibreglass panelling. The foliated capitals, the leaf-fronded cast-iron pillars and the tracery of the high-domed sheds that once adorned John Betjeman's 'cathedrals of the Railway Age' are only occasionally visible now. Modern British Rail decoration is the end of a line.

Town hall and municipal building architecture also belongs to the twilight heyday before the First World War. Middlesex Guildhall in Parliament Square, finished in 1913, and County Hall on the South Bank, not completed until 1922 and now abandoned, are dignified and impressive examples by designers who believed that public buildings were for show as much as use and snould have, as Sir Aston Webb advocated, interiors with wide, plain corridors so that people could find their way around without too many directions. Dozens of impressive-looking, late Victorian and Edwardian council headquarters and court houses in such places as Clerkenwell, Deptford, Finsbury and Shoreditch adhere to these principles.

The loss of so many homes in the City and the West End has altered the inherent character of London for all time, but the guardians of our heritage have ensured that the fabric of historically or architecturally important private houses and public buildings will be preserved for future generations: 34,420 buildings had been listed in the thirty-three boroughs of London by the end of 1992.

CHAPTER 5

Rural London

LONDON IS A GREEN CITY, a metropolis of parks and squares and tranquil open spaces that contrast with 'the huge world which roars hard by'. A pedestrian determined to walk from the palace in Kensington to Parliament at Westminster is able to get there almost entirely on a rural route, passing lakes and hollows, bridle paths, wildlife refuges, rolling lawns and formal gardens. It is a journey which goes through four royal parks—Kensington Gardens, Hyde Park, Green Park and St James's Park.

The oldest and prettiest, St James's, is also the most royal, its palaces and royal residences gazing out on the tall plane trees of The Mall. It is a park which changes dramatically in each season. The creation of this peaceful sanctuary in a bustling city has been achieved over many centuries. The deer nursery that Henry VIII established in the grounds of the old leper hospital of St James's has long since gone, and the crocodiles and menagerie kept by James I went to the royal zoo at the Tower, though his aviary is remembered by Birdcage Walk. But descendants of the ducks and strange birds given to Charles II remain. The restored King replaced trees cut down for firewood during the Civil War and, inspired by the transformation achieved by Louis XIV's gardener Le Nôtre at Versailles, he had the park laid out with walks and flower beds, and little pools linked to form the Long Canal. The King liked to stroll in the park with his dogs, feeding the ducks and such exotic birds as the pelicans given to him by the Russian ambassador. Thirty ostriches presented by a Moroccan diplomat, Evelyn noted, caused much royal amusement.

In Queen Anne's reign, as many as three hundred and fifty lime trees were planted in St James's; and in the nineteenth century great changes were effected in the landscaping of the park when John Nash, at the

LEFT: *In 1722, the royal physician Sir Hans Sloane (1660–1753) gave the Apothecaries' the freehold of the garden on condition they supplied the Royal Society with fifty specimens a year. Sloane's statue by Michael Rysbrach (a replica since 1983 when the original was removed to the British Museum) is surrounded by what John Evelyn called 'the collection of innumerable rarities'. Evelyn, himself a keen gardener, was very impressed with the heated greenhouse he inspected in 1685.*

RIGHT: *St James's Park, one of London's 'lungs', is a park for all seasons. In spring, blossom and bulbs give it colour; in summer, bright plants contrast with many shades of green. Several rare Chinese trees with dark glossy leaves and a mass of white flowers in early autumn, add, in places, an Oriental flavour. Some trees planted soon after the Restoration still stand. Queen Anne's master gardener, Henry Wise, in a bid to discourage riff-raff, persuaded her to introduce regulations in the park: no one could walk on the grass or wear clogs; the wildfowl were not to be disturbed; no trading was allowed (commercial vehicles are banned even today from The Mall); and housewives were forbidden to lay out their linen to dry.*

instigation of George IV, turned the Long Canal into the gently curving tranquil waterway that now runs between Buckingham Palace and Duck Island.

Nash also created a *rus in urbe* on Crown land at Marylebone. The outer eccentric circle of Henry VIII's hunting ground he edged with palatial terraces, and 'country house' villas loosely scattered on the inner ring were screened by small plantations. A canal, planned to cut across Regent's Park, was, at the insistence of the Crown Commissioners, diverted round the perimeter, so the story goes, lest the delicate ears of affluent residents be offended by bargees' language. Twenty-two acres were excavated for the artificial boating lake and other land leased to the London Zoological Society and the Royal Botanical Society. The royal menagerie at the Tower was transferred to the former and the gardens, the site of spectacular summer shows until this century, were renamed Queen Mary's Gardens after George V's wife who took a keen interest in their future.

RIGHT: *The* cottage ornée, *designed by the now forgotten architect, John Burges Watson, in the tradition of Nash's rustic villas, was placed on Duck Island in St James's Park by the Ornithological Society of London in 1840. It is curiously incongruous to find such a rural retreat immediately opposite the mighty Foreign and Commonweath Office. On the site formerly was the Decoy where John Evelyn once saw a one-legged crane that had been fitted with a wooden leg. Duck Island and the Decoy were created at the east end of the Long Water in 1662, but only the island survived 'Capability' Brown's alterations in 1770. Nash, too, retained the island when he reshaped the lake, giving it an uneven outline. All year, waterfowl —over forty different species— inhabit the lake and Duck Island.*

LEFT AND RIGHT: *The strict regulations that applied in St James's Park did not prevent undesirable ruffians from frequenting it. In 1712, Dean Swift complained he had to come home early 'to avoid the Mohocks', rowdy young men who contemporaries were led to believe were named after cannibals in India'! Standards of behaviour improved in the nineteenth century when it was suggested that park benches be installed and soldiers admitted. Queen Victoria took a personal interest in any such changes and once, when she heard the railings on Birdcage Walk had been moved without consulting her, she rebuked the official responsible. The proposal to allow boating on the lake was, fortunately for the ducks and geese, not adopted.*

RIGHT: *About 30,000 rose bushes make up the brilliant display in the rosary at Queen Mary's Gardens in Regent's Park. The massed profusion resembles 'carpet-bedding', a planting favoured by the Victorians and Edwardians who considered it a show of wealth. The gardens were once leased by the Royal Botanic Society who planted the borders and conservatories with many unusual species, including a banana plant from which Queen Victoria tasted the fruit for the first time. A lack of funds forced the Society to disband in 1932 after almost 100 years. The land came into the care of the Royal Parks Department and, as a gesture of thanks to George V's wife, who had been concerned about their future, the circular gardens were given her name. In spite of protests, they were re-laid out: the colourful results can be seen today.*

RIGHT: *The twelfth-century monk William Fitz-Stephen described seeing 'wooded glades and lairs of wild beasts, deer both red and fallow, wild bulls and boars' in the Great Forest of Middlesex. This was the Crown land in Marylebone that John Nash transformed into Regent's Park. Eight hundred years later, the glades are still here and so too are the wild animals, though the former are intentional landscaping features and the beasts live in some comfort in the Zoological Gardens. Besides the arbours and resting places for visitors, the Rose Garden has a small ornamental lake with a miniature island, a sanctuary for wildfowl. In summer, small boats are allowed to glide along the larger lake in the main park.*

Queen Mary was not the first consort to concern herself with the royal parks. Two centuries earlier, Caroline of Anspach, George II's wife, had been responsible for the pathway known as the Queen's Walk in the aptly named Green Park, but her more imaginative and lasting landscaping was in Hyde Park and Kensington Gardens. She had wide avenues of trees planted and introduced that landscaping illusion, the ha-ha, so the vista would not be spoilt. Outside Kensington Palace, her grand promenade, the Broad Walk, was fifty feet across and bordered by elms, which were lost in the 1950s. A basin was filled with water to become the Round Pond. Like the lakes in other royal parks, it immediately attracted waterfowl, though the geese that migrated from St James's in the 1730s were not welcomed. They pecked holes in the paths and had to be shot.

Queen Caroline's most ambitious undertaking—conceived before Lancelot 'Capability' Brown or Humphry Repton 'countrified' the great estates—was to take up a fashion set by her protégés, Charles Bridgman and William Kent. She wanted a natural look: to achieve it she had the Westbourne dammed and small ponds joined to create the Long Water in Kensington Gardens and the Serpentine in Hyde Park. Her considerable talent for designing gardens was recognized by foreign potentates who sent gifts to stock her parks: the Doge of Genoa gave her tortoises, and the Queen herself introduced red squirrels.

At the time that Queen Caroline was occupied with the royal parks and the noble landlords had begun planting the squares of their West End estates, the City was covering its few open spaces with buildings. Although it could, just, accommodate Hyde Park and Kensington Gardens (it is 60 acres larger), the City is today a green-free zone where collective blades of grass are a rare commodity. It has remained unchanged for centuries, though William Fitz-Stephen noticed in 1174 that some houses had gardens 'well furnished with trees, spacious and beautiful', and Ralph Treswell's surveys of c.1600 show lawns behind more sizeable Tudor houses. The less well-off had to relax on 'the great fen or moor' where Fitz-Stephen had seen children skating in winter. Part of this former swamp at Moorgate, a public area in the fifteenth century, became the City's first park when 'the lower walks of Moorfields' were left to it in 1605 'for the use and enjoyment of the

RIGHT: *An avenue of bay trees, clipped holly and hawthorn bushes shelter the lawn and Orangery in Kensington Gardens from the pleached lime arbour enclosing the palace's sunken garden, an Edwardian replacement for one created for Queen Anne. The Queen always came to Kensington Palace at Easter and, with the help of Henry Wise, extended the gardens around her home, though it was Caroline of Anspach who dictated most of the present layout. The baroque redbrick Orangery was designed for Anne by Sir John Vanbrugh, possibly with help from Nicholas Hawksmoor. The interior, with carvings by Grinling Gibbons and remarkable statuary, is very fine, and here she took tea and gave supper parties. She also tried to grow oranges, but without success.*

P·C·HAROLD FRANK RICKETTS
METROPOLITAN POLICE

DROWNED AT TEIGNMOUTH
WHILST TRYING TO RESCUE
A BOY BATHING AND SEEN
TO BE IN DIFFICULTY
· 11 SEPT · 1916 ·

P·C·EDWARD GEORGE·
BROWN GREENOFF
METROPOLITAN POLICE
MANY LIVES WERE SAVED BY HIS
DEVOTION TO DUTY AT THE
TERRIBLE EXPLOSION AT
SILVERTOWN · 19·JAN·1917·

P·C·PERCY EDWIN COOK
METROPOLITAN POLICE
VOLUNTARILY DESCENDED HIGH
TENSION CHAMBER AT KENSINGTON
TO RESCUE TWO WORKMEN
OVERCOME BY POISONOUS GAS
· 7 OCT · 1927 ·

FREDERICK MILLS A. RUTTER
ROBERT DURRANT & F·D·JONES
WHO LOST THEIR LIVES IN
BRAVELY STRIVING TO SAVE
A COMRADE AT THE SEWAGE
PUMPING WORKS · EAST HAM
JULY 1ST · 1895 ·

ELIZABETH BOXALL
AGED 17 of BETHNAL GREEN
WHO DIED OF INJURIES RECEIVED
IN TRYING TO SAVE
A CHILD
FROM A RUNAWAY HORSE
JUNE · 20 · 1888 ·

HERBERT PETER CAZALY
STATIONER'S CLERK
WHO WAS DROWNED AT KEW
IN ENDEAVOURING TO SAVE
A MAN FROM DROWNING
APRIL 21 1889

·HERBERT MACONOGHU·
SCHOOL BOY FROM WIMBLEDON AGED 13
· HIS PARENTS ABSENT IN INDIA, LOST ·
HIS LIFE IN VAINLY TRYING TO RESCUE
· HIS TWO SCHOOL FELLOWS WHO WERE ·
· DROWNED AT GLOVERS POOL, CROYDE,
NORTH DEVON · AUGUST · 28 · 1882 ·

SAMUEL RABBETH
MEDICAL OFFICER
OF THE ROYAL FREE HOSPITAL
WHO TRIED TO SAVE A CHILD
SUFFERING FROM DIPHTHERIA
AT THE COST OF HIS OWN LIFE
OCTOBER 26 · 1884 ·

FREDERICK ALFRED CROFT
INSPECTOR · AGED 31
SAVED A LUNATIC WOMAN
FROM SUICIDE AT WOOLWICH
ARSENAL STATION · BUT WAS
HIMSELF RUN OVER BY THE TRAIN
· JAN · 11 · 1878 ·

HARRY SISLEY OF
KILBURN AGED 10
DROWNED IN ATTEMPTING
TO SAVE HIS BROTHER
AFTER HE HIMSELF HAD
JUST BEEN RESCUED
MAY 1878

JAMES HEWERS
1878
KILLED BY A TRAIN
AT RICHMOND IN THE
ENDEAVOUR TO SAVE
ANOTHER MAN

GEORGE ELLIOTT
AGED 10
WHEN A FRIEND BATHING IN
WENT TO HIS RESCUE
AND WAS DROWNED

LEFT: *The tiny garden between Little Britain and St Martin's le Grand is known as Postman's Park for the very good reason that it was beside the General Post Office. In the shelter, a remarkable gallery of memorial tablets commemorate heroic deeds of self-sacrifice. The idea came from the artist G. F. Watts who wrote a letter to* The Times *in 1877 suggesting that 'names worthy to be remembered' should not be forgotten. Most of the simple inscriptions ('Thomas Simpson died of exhaustion after saving many lives from the breaking ice at Highgate Ponds, Jan 25 1885', for example) tell moving stories of perilous acts.*

LEFT: *The garden of Postman's Park was formerly the churchyard of St Botolph's, Aldersgate, and two other churches, and the gravestones are now lined up against a wall.*

Citizens' by two sisters, Mary and Cathrine Fynnes. Finsbury Circus, the only 'lung' with breathing space in the City, is their legacy.

Except for Charterhouse, the monastery gardens have disappeared and buildings have encroached on the formally planted Drapers' Gardens where the fashionable came to promenade in the eighteenth century. Only a privileged few can enjoy the verdant Garden Court hidden deep in the Bank of England, and the gardens at the Temple, where Shakespeare's Richard Plantagenet and the Earl of Somerset plucked the symbolic red and white roses of the Wars of the Roses, are also private. The memorial gardens by Tower Hill, with their grisly associations, are small, and Postman's Park—so called because the General Post Office was beside it—was laid out on land that once belonged to three churches. It and dozens of churchyards are now small oases in mountainous ranges of office blocks.

The City Fathers may not have been prepared to yield open space within the Square Mile, but they did acquire land for public amenities beyond the bounds. Epping Forest, almost 500 acres in Surrey and Burnham Beeches are in their care and in recent years they have assumed responsibility for Hampstead Heath.

RIGHT: *A seventeenth-century garden, which the Marchioness of Salisbury helped to plant in the 1980s, thrives in the churchyard of St Mary-at-Lambeth, and a museum devoted to garden history is being assembled in the church. Many of the flowers, trees and shrubs, such as honeysuckle and a Judas tree, were introduced to England and propagated by the Tradescant family, gardeners to James I, Charles I and Robert Cecil, the first Earl of Salisbury. They travelled widely to collect botanical specimens; John, the father, brought fruit trees from Holland and Flanders, gladiolus byzantinus and the African marigold from Spain and North Africa, and angelica and the Siberian larch from Russia. His son, also John, went on three expeditions to North America, returning with columbines, a tulip tree and Virginia creeper.*

RIGHT: *Two sarcophagi stand in the garden at St Mary-at-Lambeth. One is the tomb of the Tradescants whose home, known as Tradescant's Ark, was nearby in south Lambeth; here they had a physic garden said to contain the most extensive plant collection in the country. This detail on the tomb shows a skull and Hydra, the seven-headed serpent of Greek mythology. The second grave is Captain Bligh's. He was on an expedition to bring back the bread fruit plant from the South Seas when the mutiny took place on the Bounty in 1789. The redundant church, which was falling into disrepair, was rescued and, because of its assocations with the Tradescants and Bligh, the decision was made to turn it into the Museum of Garden History.*

Many individual aldermen and Lord Mayors followed Westminster's landed gentry into the country and bought estates which, because of a need to be near the City, were often on the fringes of London. A considerable number of these parklands survive. Abandoned and no longer in family ownership, they are now carefully tended public parks, schools, colleges or religious houses.

A glance at outer London reveals that in Bexley John Champneis, a Lord Mayor, built Hall Place in 1537; nearby, John Boyd, a director of the East India Company, had the grounds around his Palladian house at Danson landscaped in the style of 'Capability' Brown. On the Essex side of the river, another East India Company man, its governor Sir Josiah Child, owned the estate that today encompasses Wanstead Park and its golf course. RAF Uxbridge and a Catholic convent are on land that surrounded a house owned by the banking family of Cox; and Ravenscourt Park was the retreat of Sir Richard Gurney, a royalist Lord Mayor. One of Ealing's 127 parks, Walpole Park, was the country seat of Sir John Soane, the antiquarian and architect of the Bank of England. Another, Gunnersbury, became the summer home of Princess Amelia who, like her mother Queen Caroline, had a way with

LEFT: *Trees and shrubs from Japan have been planted to spectacular effect in the Royal Botanic Gardens at Kew. Great cedars and specimens of* Cupressus obtusa *rise in clusters amid the 288 acres. Kew is, of course, a scientific research centre whose single, most important contribution to the Empire occurred when Henry A. Wickham, a resident in Brazil, was asked to return post-haste with as many seeds of* Hevea brasiliensis *as he could bring. He bowled up to Kew in a hansom cab in June 1876 with 70,000, which were immediately sown. Two months later, about 1,900 seedlings were dispatched to Ceylon, and from these the great rubber industry of the Far East grew.*

LEFT: *The Carthusian monks at Charterhouse, the monastery in Clerkenwell, led solitary lives, according to the rules of the order. Each had his own cell and a tiny garden in which personal taste was followed. During the Dissolution, when many of the monks were hanged at Tyburn, the gardens were plundered by servants of the King and Richard Cromwell: they removed bay trees, rosemary grafts and fruit trees. The monastery became home to several noble families before Thomas Sutton bought it in 1611 as a school for boys (today sited at Godalming in Surrey) and an almshouse for elderly gentlemen (which survives).*

gardens and also employed William Kent. Later, the Rothschilds, a family whose contribution to horticulture has been as important as their financial acumen, came to Gunnersbury. And at Osterley, the pre-Adam house and park belonged to Sir Thomas Gresham, founder of the Royal Exchange.

In the botanical world, Kew Gardens have been of exceptional importance for more than two hundred years. Like other large parks, they were once two estates. Again, Queen Caroline played a role. She and George II bought the Richmond Lodge estate in 1721, and with Charles Bridgman, who worked with her in Hyde Park, 'dared to introduce cultivated fields, and even morsels of forest appearance', according to Horace Walpole. William Kent built her a grotto and Merlin's Cave, 'a thatched Edifice, and very Gothique'. As it housed six wax figures modelled on recognizable servants and courtiers, it caused a great deal of comment. The planting and development of Kew were continued by her son Frederick, who, Walpole records, 'began great works in the garden', and by his widow, Augusta, Princess of Wales.

LEFT AND RIGHT: *Hampstead Heath (left) and Epping Forest (right), though some way from the Square Mile, are in the care of the City of London. Epping, once a royal hunting ground stretching into Essex, started to be enclosed by local farmers in the last century. This loss of land and the growing number of trees being lopped for firewood—producing today's pollarded beeches—gave rise to concern, and an Act of Parliament in 1878 granted the forest to the City of London. The 6,000 acres, declared an open space for 'the enjoyment of my people forever' by Queen Victoria, have many species of trees: hornbeams are especially plentiful. A lake, ponds, bridle paths and great clumps of trees make it, and Hampstead Heath, welcome green spaces in the sprawling capital. The Heath was preserved in perpetuity for the public at about the same time as Epping, when building threatened to encroach on its 800 acres.*

The Physic Garden, the Arboretum and the first great glasshouse were among Augusta's improvements and she also accepted the gift of a rare collection of shrubs and trees from Whitton Park at Twickenham after the Duke of Argyll's death. Some of these old trees still stand in the Royal Botanic Gardens.

A few outlying estates have become twentieth-century parks, and the heaths have been protected by law; but in inner suburbs the farms and grass meadows of Islington or Lambeth were sacrificed for homes for London's fast-growing population. But, in leaving behind crowded tenements and smoky rookeries, the city dweller yearned for small reminders of the rural pastures that had once been there, and had a small garden put behind his new house. These are now the thousand upon thousands of tiny gardens that lie hidden behind endless ranks of terraced houses all over London. Often beautifully, and certainly lovingly, cultivated, they are a lasting proof of the Englishman's passion for gardens and, like the great parks, they are London's pride.

CHAPTER 6

London Pleasures

LONDON HAS A VITALITY unmatched by few other capitals, a diversity of pleasures and pastimes which have hardly changed in hundreds of years. The modern attractions are somewhat similar to those that brought Mrs Purefoys, the widow of a well-to-do Buckinghamshire squire, and her son, Henry, on a fourteen-hour coach journey from rural Shalstone in 1749. During an eleven-day stay, this indomitable seventy-six-year-old shopped and went to all the 'sights'. In one June day alone she saw her silversmith and two other tradesmen in the morning, entertained friends to luncheon, inspected St Stephen Walbrook, the Bank of England, South Sea House (now gone), Guildhall and Moorfields before taking in Westminster Abbey. The Tower of London, where the lions caught her attention, and a trip by boat to see the splendours of Greenwich occupied another day.

Had Mrs Purefoys arrived in London six weeks earlier, she could have seen the pageantry to mark the Treaty of Aix-la-Chapelle in Green Park, and she might have gone to the pleasure gardens at Vauxhall to the rehearsal of the *Music for the Royal Fireworks*, commissioned by George II for the huge celebration. Over 12,000 people paid to listen to Handel's music, the crowd so big that it took over three hours to cross London Bridge. In the six days that followed, thousands thronged Piccadilly to see the elaborate rococo Temple of Peace which, at 410 feet long and 114 feet high, had been built to hold an orchestra of one hundred musicians. The wooden structure also secreted cannons to be fired during the overture, and 10,000 rockets to accompany the music. At 8.30 p.m. on 27 April 1749, the King, the Court, the thousands who had paid to sit in the stands and a vast number of sightseers heard the orchestra striking up. The cannons boomed, rockets flew in all directions and, to the dismay of all, the wooden Temple burst into

LEFT: *Simpsons-in-the-Strand is a restaurant with a reputation for traditional British food. The famous Victorian chef Alex Soyer suggested serving sides of beef and saddles of mutton from a dinner waggon, an idea which has withstood over 100 years of food fads.*

ABOVE: *Shops, eating houses and places of entertainment used to line the Strand. Among them could be found a barbershop-singing mouse, an elephant named 'Chunee' in the menagerie at Exeter Change, poses plastiques—nearly nude girls in classical drapes—and the Academy of Vocal Music and the Madrigal Society, which met at the Crown and Anchor. The Grand Cigar Divan, a Regency establishment where men played chess in booths, was the business John Simpson, a caterer, joined in 1848. He rebuilt the premises and began serving his now legendary traditional luncheons.*

flames. The malicious pen of the gossip Horace Walpole noted, a little unfairly, that 'the fireworks by no means answered the expense, the length of preparation and expectation that had been raised. The rockets and whatever was thrown into the air succeeded mighty well but the wheels, and all that was to compose the principal part, were pitiful.'

The King's peace celebrations were a diversion in a city not overflowing with amusements for the majority of people. Ten years before the Purefoys' visit, Maitland's *History of London* recorded 515 coffee houses in the City and West End, 207 inns, 447 taverns, 5,975 beer houses and, significantly, 8,659 brandy shops. The tax on English brandy was small. Mixed with the essence of juniper berries and sold as 'geneva' or gin by innumerable shopkeepers, it was a cheap, potent elixir which made men and women who were barely able to afford food and clothes temporarily forget their troubles; children were given nips to stop them crying. Hogarth's *Gin Lane* and *A Rake's Progress* are

LEFT: *British weather can run from winter to summer in an afternoon, and an umbrella, or parasol, is a vital accessory in a Londoner's daily equipage. James Smith recognized this when he set up shop in 1830: the firm's longevity is proof of his business acumen. It is the oldest, and the largest, umbrella shop in Europe. His son's vision stretched further. When he moved to 53 New Oxford Street twenty-seven years later, he saw the wisdom in making their own umbrellas, and a workshop was installed above the shop. Ceremonial maces, used in London's pageants, and regimental 'swagger' canes are also a speciality of the firm.*

LEFT: *Floris is probably the oldest shop in London still owned by the same family, and still on the same site. The directors are descended from Juan Famenias Floris, a barber from Minorca, who opened his shop in Jermyn Street in 1730. The pomades and fragrances he created, a novelty at the time, quickly gained favour, and every sovereign since George IV has granted Floris a royal warrant. The vaults, built in 1675, are still used today to store perfumes, before they are transferred to the gleaming Spanish mahogany showcases which the Floris family acquired at the Great Exhibition in 1851.*

LEFT: *Today all spic and span, with the iron arches and pilasters freshly painted and the vaulted glass roofs renovated, Leadenhall Market in the City has taken on a new lease of life. Smart wine bars, restaurants and delicatessens now mingle with the fishmongers, butchers and game and poultry sellers who have been purveying produce in it since the fourteenth century when 'foreigners' (meaning anyone from outside London) were allowed in to sell poultry, butter and cheese. When Sir Horace Jones, the City architect, rebuilt the market in 1881, he retained the medieval street pattern. At that time, remains of the Roman basilica were found underneath and a tessellated pavement, now in the British Museum, shows an inebriated Bacchus happily riding on a tiger.*

LEFT: *Covent Garden became a centre of nightlife early in the eighteenth century. The aristocracy had moved west and their houses were taken over as coffee houses, taverns and bagnios, provoking Sir John Fielding, the Bow Street magistrate, to remark that 'One would imagine all the prostitutes in the Kingdom had picked upon the neighbourhood for a general rendezvous . . .' There were twenty-four gaming houses, and Harris's* Man of Pleasure's Kalendar *for 1773 lists the physical attributes and addresses of 170 'Covent-Garden Ladies'. The fruit, vegetable and flower market, which had operated since 1674, expanded to become the biggest in England. After it moved in 1974, the covered halls, erected in the 1830s, were restored to house shops, wine bars, restaurants and a central bazaar. Buskers today entertain passers-by in the piazza where in May 1662 Pepys watched a Punch and Judy show.*

RIGHT: *Charles Dickens once invited his friend John Forster to take a brisk walk with him over Hampstead Heath where he knew 'a good 'ouse where we can have a red-hot chop for dinner, and a glass of good wine'—Jack Straw's Castle. Legend insists that Jack Straw, the executed rebel leader who opposed the poll tax in 1381, hid here after he burned down the Priory of St John in Clerkenwell but the name is more likely to derive from an old generic term for a rustic. The inn's origins are obscure but it is known to have existed in 1714. The present building was reconstructed in 1961 after World War II bomb damage.*

RIGHT: *Southwark was beyond legal reach of the City and consequently abounded with playhouses, baiting pits, brothels and alehouses. As the only galleried inn left in London, the George has achieved an importance today that it never had in previous centuries when a number of medieval inns lined Southwark High Street. The neighbouring Tabard, where Chaucer's pilgrims slept in 'chambers wyde' before departing to Canterbury, was far more famous. The tradition of open-air theatre has been carried into this century and occasionally plays by Shakespeare have been performed in the yard.*

not exaggerations of social life in London then. Two of the latter series, painted in 1732–3 (now in Sir John Soane's Museum), show dissipated drunks and loose women at an orgy in the Rose Tavern in Covent Garden; and 'The Gaming House' is set in White's, a coffee house (and forerunner of today's respectable Conservative Club) in which the gaming tables are frequented by gamblers, cheats and moneylenders.

The entertainments best enjoyed by the people were at the annual fairs, whose modern successors are to be discovered on Blackheath or Hampstead Heath on spring or summer public holidays. Large numbers flocked to the May Fair in Shepherd's Market, to Southwark Fair and to Smithfield where the greatest of London's fairs, the Bartholomew Fair, had been held since Henry I granted it a charter in 1123. Although it had become (with the May Fair) rowdy, noisy and filled with cutpurses early in the eighteenth century, it gave poorer people the chance to see jugglers, conjurors, exhibitions of freaks and monsters, comedians and showmen. Its heyday was in Jacobean times, when Ben Jonson immortalized it in his portrait of Londoners on a spree, but by 1855 it had become so disorderly and raffish that the City closed it down.

BELOW: *The slightly old-fashioned sign on the arcade in front of the hotel César Ritz built in Piccadilly in 1906 is no preparation for the very French* beaux arts *splendours of the restaurant. Mirrored walls, chandeliers, swags of gilded flowers and the* trompe l'oeil *sky painting on the ceiling combine to make dining at the Ritz a grand occasion.*

In winter, if the Thames froze over, the fairground folk migrated to the river where innkeepers set up stalls on the ice for what John Evelyn described in 1684 as a 'bacchanalian triumph'. Booths 'full of commodities' were laid out like streets across the river, and puppet shows, football and coach racing were organized. The last of these spasmodic fairs was in 1813–14.

The plays by Ben Jonson and his contemporaries were performed in an era when more liberal attitudes towards theatre prevailed. Four hundred years earlier, when the monk who was Thomas à Becket's clerk, William Fitz-Stephen, wrote about 'dramatic performances of a more sacred kind', he was referring to plays put on by priests to illustrate the Gospels to people unable to read or write. As monks were not usually allowed to leave their monasteries, the guilds assumed responsibility for the performances which, known as Mystery Plays (because each guild referred to its trade by the word 'Mystery', a corruption from the Latin word for 'occupation'), were taken round the city and performed from the back of carts in marketplaces and in the courtyards of inns.

Gradually, the Miracle and Morality Plays became more elaborate. Stow, who had examined the records of the guilds, or livery companies, for his *Survey*, said an epic attended by 'most of the nobility and gentry of England' in 1409 took eight days, a feat of endurance not yet attempted by even such experimental modern directors as Peter Hall, Trevor Nunn or Michael Bogdanov.

Travelling minstrels played for bed and board at inns, where pilgrims would also frequently stay the night. These hostelries were very often closely associated with churches, the wardens of which were, in many instances, the brewers.

The Church and the City of London waged a continual war against plays of a non-religious kind and tried to clamp down on frivolous entertainment, especially if performed on a public stage. But they could not invade the Court, where masques with singing, dancing and dialogue were given privately, or the great city houses of noblemen who, in the sixteenth century, maintained companies of players.

Shortly after the Reformation, when there was a growing band of travelling players, Queen Mary ordered all 'strolling' to cease because it

RIGHT: *From the Restoration until 1843 only three theatres in London were licensed to put on plays—the Theatres Royal at Drury Lane and Covent Garden and, in the summer months, the younger Theatre Royal, Haymarket. Things were very different in Shakespeare's time, when there were at least seventeen theatres; today, there are more than forty. At the time of its centenary in 1820, the Haymarket was completely rebuilt at a cost of £20,000 to designs by John Nash. The Victorian policy of presenting classic comedies and plays with star names still continues. Most actors asked to name their favourite theatre will choose the Haymarket. With its handsome portico, lovely old-gold auditorium, and comfortable dressing rooms, it is easy to appreciate why it is a popular choice.*

LEFT AND RIGHT: Amorini *perched on the London Coliseum hold festoons above cartouches on the tower. At the base of the Corinthian columns on the rotunda (right) are four great statues representing Music, Art, Literature and Science. Lions, each with a paw placed on a ball, once looked down from the platforms below the globe but were removed some forty years ago. However, the pairs of golden lions drawing chariots across the top of stage boxes in the gloriously ornate auditorium still gaze down on audiences. Frank Matcham, the architect who designed the theatre, decorated the interior with mosaics, polished alabaster and elaborate, colourful plaster work. Shields and torch-like light fittings were intended to evoke the spirit of the Roman Colosseum, considered in ancient days the greatest place of entertainment in existence.*

LEFT: *The Coliseum in St Martin's Lane was the idea of the impresario Sir Oswald Stoll who hoped the largest and most luxurious theatre in his empire would be 'as worthy of London today as the ancient amphitheatre of Vespasian was of Rome'. From its opening in 1904, until it became a cinema in the 1950s, the greatest singers, dancers, actors, clowns and vaudevillians of the century appeared at this palace of varieties. Pavlova, Sarah Bernhardt, Grock, the clown, and Sir Henry Wood have all taken curtain calls. In 1968, the Coliseum became the home of the English National Opera. Stoll, who engaged Decima Moore to sing on the opening night and later gave a promising young tenor, John McCormack, top billing, would heartily approve of the packed houses that nightly fill the magnificent theatre to hear today's opera stars.*

was feared the actors would spread heresy and treason. A company appearing in a play called *A Sack full of News* at the Boar's Head Inn, outside Aldgate, was briefly imprisoned and told in future all plays had to be approved by the Privy Council. (In more recent times, the Lord Chamberlain had the power to censor all plays, a situation which lasted until 1968.)

Like the Church, which thought actors 'an idle sort of people, who have been infamous in all good communities', the Court of Common Council imposed restrictions and insisted anyone who wanted to produce a play must obtain a licence from the Lord Mayor. But the Court had no jurisdiction over the liberties (the districts immediately outside the walls), and it was in the northern liberty of Shoreditch that James Burbage, an actor in the Earl of Leicester's Company, leased a plot of land in 1576.

Shoreditch was close to the City and Burbage reckoned the Theatre, as it was known, would attract the public and companies under the patronage of noblemen. He was right, and within a year the Curtain had opened nearby. In due course they merged, and companies such as the Lord Chamberlain's Men, joined in about 1594 by William Shakespeare who was then a young actor, performed in both playhouses.

Meanwhile, on Bankside, Philip Henslowe, a businessman and promoter of the company known as the Lord Admiral's Men, had built a circular theatre to which large audiences were drawn to see his future stepson-in-law, the actor Edward Alleyn. They came to see his *Dr Faustus* and *Tamburlaine*, two new plays by the young wonder boy, Kit Marlowe. This was the Rose—to re-emerge spectacularly in the spring of 1989 during an archaeological dig, more than 380 years after it had disappeared.

The Rose was quickly followed by the Swan, the Hope and the Globe, the most famous theatre of all in which many of Shakespeare's plays were originally performed. The Globe had been built soon after the lease of the Theatre fell due in 1598. Burbage's men dismantled the playhouse and carted the timbers across the Thames to be reused in the new theatre. This was probably the 'wooden O' Shakespeare referred to in the prologue of *Henry V*, which may have been the first of his plays to be seen here.

RIGHT: *Music (in particular, the Promenade Concerts begun by the conductor Sir Henry Wood) is the performing art most associated with the Royal Albert Hall. Ironically, acoustics have been a recurring problem and an echo once caused the conductor Sir Thomas Beecham to say that this was the only place a British composer could hear his works played twice! Built as the Hall of Arts and Sciences, but named after the Prince Consort by Queen Victoria when it opened in 1871, the huge amphitheatre is frequently converted for tennis and boxing tournaments, or used for dance spectaculars, balls or conventions. Every summer, London's greatest annual festival of music—the Proms—attracts up to 8,000 music lovers a night to hear orchestras, chamber ensembles, choirs and singers from all over the world.*

The great days of the theatre on Bankside lasted into the seventeenth century. The Globe, destroyed in 1613 when cannons used during *Henry VIII* set the thatch on fire, was quickly replaced and survived until it was eventually shut down in the 1640s by the Puritans. Its exact location was uncertain until, like the Rose, the outline of the structure was uncovered by archaeologists from the Museum of London in 1989.

During the Restoration in 1660, plays were revived due to Charles II's love of theatre. He granted patents which gave Thomas Killigrew and Sir William Davenant a quasi-monopoly on legitimate drama in London. The Theatre Royal, Drury Lane, which staged plays by Killigrew, William Wycherley and Thomas Otway, operated under licence; and from 1732, when the Davenant patent was transferred from the Lincoln's Inn Theatre, so did the Theatre Royal, Covent Garden (today's Royal Opera House). The Haymarket, which had flouted the law for over forty years, was granted a licence in 1766 for the summer months. The patents, which still carry certain privileges, remained in force until an Act of Parliament in 1843 regulated a situation in which a growing band of actor-managers had been unofficially mounting productions for years.

Performances, which had flourished at the patent playhouses, increased and many new theatres were built—twenty-two between 1880 and 1914, ten between 1928 and 1931. Today, more than forty theatres of consequence spill out of the West End into the City and across the river to the South Bank. Smaller theatres proliferate in fringe areas; a few, like the King's Head and the Red Lion in Islington, are pubs that carry on the tradition of producing plays and entertainments in inns.

The Hope, the Bankside theatre of Shakespeare's day, where *Bartholomew Fair* was first seen in 1614, was a baiting arena before Philip Henslow converted it, and for some years it alternated as a playhouse and bear-baiting pit. Bull and bear-baiting, popular winter pastimes for centuries, continued well into the eighteenth century, their attraction slowly diminishing until a law against them was enforced in 1835; though, like dog-fighting, clandestine fights continued. Cock-fighting also attracted crowds and Fitz-Stephen recalled that it was the custom on Shrove Tuesday for boys to bring fighting cocks into the classroom where they 'indulged all the morning'.

Although warlike jousting tournaments and many other dangerous sports have died out (the mock naval battles on the Thames, for example, which were watched by large crowds at London Bridge; and the perilous games of armed combat played out on the frozen ponds at Moorfields wearing ice-skates made of animal bones), such medieval games as wrestling, stone-throwing and 'slinging javelins beyond a mark' have survived as Olympic sports, along with the commonest of all, archery. While hunting is not possible in London today, almost every able-bodied man in previous centuries took falcons, hawks and dogs into the woods close to the City or even further away in Fitz-Stephen's time, when Londoners had hunting rights in 'Middlesex, Hartfordshire, all Chiltron, and in Kent to the water of Cray.'

Today's young people, like their ancestors, play with bats and balls and do so in fields and parks, unlike the generation whose pitch was the aisle of old St Paul's. This caused Bishop Braybrook in 1385 to ban 'the playing of ball' in the Cathedral, but to no avail.

LEFT: *Several public houses have stood on the site occupied by the Salisbury, which gets its name from the Victorian Prime Minister, the third Marquess of Salisbury, a descendant of Sir Robert Cecil who bought land in St Martin's Lane in 1609. Ben Caunt, the prize fighter after whom 'Big Ben' is possibly called, ran an earlier tavern here in the middle of the last century.*

LEFT: *The saloon bar door, windows and interior partitions of the Salisbury are all of ornate engraved glass. Inside, the dark wood counter overlaid with pink, streaked marble, the brass fittings and the curvaceous lampholders between yellow button-backed seating combine to give the late Victorian pub the flavour of a gin palace. The raffish atmosphere is accentuated by the knowledge that it was a haunt of the flamboyant defector, Guy Burgess.*

LEFT: *St Katharine's Dock is today a marina for yachts and pleasure craft. The Victorian warehouses have been transformed into offices and residences, with restaurants, pubs and shops at street level. For 700 years, a charitable organization was here. The Royal Foundation of St Katharine, established by Queen Mathilda in 1148, cared for the sick and gave hospitality to foreigners forbidden to enter the City. All queens consort were directly responsible for it, and, because of the intervention of Catherine of Aragon, St Katharine's survived the Dissolution of the Monasteries. In 1825, when England had no queen, the hospital moved and the premises were redeveloped as a dock designed by Thomas Telford.*

LEFT: *Ivory, a valuable import from the East, was landed and stored in the Ivory House (far right) at St Katharine's Dock in the last century. A pair of trumpeting elephants with ivory tusks stand sentinel on the East Smithfield entrance to the former dock. Elephants have always intrigued Londoners. When King Louis IX of France sent one to Henry III, crowds flocked to see it in a specially built house at the Tower of London. Unfortunately, the elephant died within two years.*

In the smaller city of long ago, 'earls, barons and knights' went to look on or buy at the weekly Smithfield horse fair where 'nags' were put through their paces somewhat in the manner of modern equestrian events. Some were raced, the spectators cheering on jockeys who, 'inspired with the love of praise and the hope of victory', showed the whip to their mounts, hoping to get to the finishing post first. Today's punter has to travel further afield to Sandown Park or Kempton Park: the short-lived early Victorian Hippodrome in Notting Hill quickly disappeared and, after 102 years, the racecourse at Alexandra Palace closed in 1970. Almost the only equestrian sports in modern London are the annual showjumping events at Olympia and Wembley, though leisurely cantering on Rotten Row is a reminder of days when London society came to be seen taking the air in Hyde Park.

Yachting on the Thames originated as a sport from a £100-stake race in 1661 between Charles II and his brother, James, Duke of York. It is rare on the tidal river today, though motor-powered craft of all sizes chug up the river to the marina in St Katharine's Dock.

Bare-knuckle fighting, not seen much since the last century, has been replaced by the gloved bouts and Queensberry rules of boxing, a sport which now brings audiences to the Café Royal or the Royal Albert Hall where musical evenings sometimes give way to another popular spectator sport—tennis. The grass courts at Wimbledon are the most famous of numerous tennis clubs in London and public courts are also to be found in parks and a growing number of leisure centres, including indoor courts for the much older game of real tennis at Lord's grounds in St John's Wood where the modern rules of lawn tennis were drawn up. Lord's is, of course, the headquarters of cricket, one of the few spectator sports within easy reach of people living in central London; and the second test-match ground, at the Oval in Kennington, is also close to Westminster.

The pleasures and pastimes that brought Mrs Purefoys and her son, Henry, to town still attract visitors from the provinces and overseas. They come to shop, to take in the sights and, with the resident Londoner, attend concerts and the theatre. They visit the museums and galleries and, at the end of the day, relax over dinner in one of the many London restaurants or enjoy the convivial atmosphere of a local pub—taking care, of course, not to give just cause for a complaint like that made by William Fitz-Stephen about 'the immoderate drinking of foolish persons'!

LEFT: *Imitate Gene Kelly performing 'Singing in the Rain' along Burlington Arcade, and a beadle will soon see that the rules of no running, singing or carrying an open umbrella are obeyed. The arcade of exclusive shops between Piccadilly and Burlington Gardens was built in 1819 to prevent passers-by tossing rubbish into the garden of Burlington House.*

LEFT: *This bust of a Greek man sits on an elaborate scroll above the Piccadilly entrance to Burlington Arcade, put there with a female companion when the arcade was given a new entrance in 1931. The arms of Lord Burlington are high over the arch. Richard, the third Earl of Burlington, built the great Palladian house (today, home of the Royal Academy of Arts and other learned societies) which adjoins the arcade.*

LEFT: *The clock over the entrance to Fortnum and Mason has two guardhouses. When the clock strikes, the doors open and the founders of the famous Piccadilly store can be seen—William Fortnum, a footman to Queen Anne and his landlord, who had a stall in St James's market.*

Red, deep-pile carpet, crystal chandeliers, assistants in morning coats and the mouthwatering aroma of delicacies convey the atmosphere of opulence that has given Fortnum and Mason its reputation for being the most luxurious store in London. The figures on the elaborate clock bow to each other on the hour. Although it has the appearance of being old, the clock was only installed in 1964.

LEFT: *Giraffes have been an attraction at London Zoo since four arrived in 1836, shortly after the royal menageries at the Tower of London and Windsor were moved to Regent's Park. The one female gave birth to six babies within five years. Today, the zoo houses many thousands of animals in environments which try to simulate the creatures' natural habitats. The appeal of exotic animals goes back to the thirteenth century when the Tower's menagerie was started with the gift of leopards and an elephant to Henry III. The King of Norway presented him with a polar bear which was allowed to go fishing in the Thames at the end of a long rope. Five hundred years later, Queen Charlotte was given the first zebra to arrive in England. She kept it in a menagerie near Buckingham House where the curious came to see it.*

Index

*Numbers in italics refer
to illustration captions*

Acknowledgements

There are so many books on London that even a brief bibliography of those consulted would run to many pages. Therefore only indispensible sources and a selection which may make interesting further reading on general or specialized aspects of London are mentioned.

London 2000 Years of a City and its People by Felix Barker and Peter Jackson (Papermac) is a 'bible', an illustrated history in which every significant event and person of importance in the development of London comes to life. The on-going volumes of *The Survey of London* are the foremost authority on the parishes so far. Since the demise of the Greater London Council, this series has been published by Athlone Press and is currently edited by Hermione Hobhouse. *London I: The Cities of London and Westminster* by Sir Nikolaus Pevsner (Penguin, revised by B. Cherry) and *The Art and Architecture of London* by Ann Saunders (Phaidon: Oxford, 1984) are valuable sources of information. *London: The Unique City* (Jonathan Cape) by Steen Eiler Rasmussen, the Danish town planner, offers a perceptive opinion on London's evolution and future. For quick reference, *The London Encyclopaedia* by B. Weinrib and C. Hibbert (Papermac) is informative.

Specialized books that have proved useful include *The Survey of London* by John Stow with new introduction by Valerie Pearl (J. Dent, 1987); *The Soul of the City: London's Livery Companies* by Colonel Robert J. Blackman (Sampson Low, Marston & Co.); *A History of London Life* by R. J. Mitchell and M. D. R. Leys (Longmans, Green and Co. 1958); *London Coffee Houses* by Bryant Lillywhite (George Allen & Unwin Ltd, 1963); *A guide to London's Churches* by M. Blatch (Constable, 1978); *London Statues: A guide to London's outdoor statues and sculpture* (Constable, 1981); *The Royal Parks of London* by Guy Williams (Constable, 1978); *London's Pride: the Glorious History of the Capital's Gardens*, edited by Mireille Galinou (Anaya Publishers Ltd, 1989); and *The London Topographical Society Record* of which twenty-six volumes of articles relating to maps and plans, and to London topography in general, have been published since the Society was founded.

Guide books such as *The Blue Guide to London*, edited by Ylva French, *London: Louise Nicholson's Definitive Guide* (The Bodley Head, 1988) and the Ordnance Survey's Landranger guide, *London and Beyond*, contain all an inquisitive visitor or resident should require.

A great number of people have given us information or arranged facilities for photography and we thank Emma St John Smith at Westminster Abbey, Elaine Collins at Guildhall, Rosemary Nicholson at the Museum of Garden History, Paul Handley at Lambeth Palace, Colonel G. A. Allan OBE, Major R. A. G. Courage and James Carruthers at the Royal Hospital, Chelsea, John Addey of Canonbury House, John Hall at the George Inn, John Proctor of Prudential Insurance (Burlington Arcade), Mrs S. M. Holyoake at Charterhouse, David Hebblethwaite at Church House and Jonathan Herbert of Chelsea for their time and friendly help.

Assistance was also willingly offered by the priests at St Sophia's and Brompton Oratory and we thank them and the directors, curators and staff at the British Museum, Natural History Museum, Chelsea Physic Garden, Somerset House, Keats' House and London Zoo, as well as the staff of Berry Bros and the Bodenham family and Amanda Farnish at J. Floris.

A number of people, who remain nameless, willingly moved their cars to enable Andrew to take unimpeded views of streets or houses, and we extend our gratitude to them.

Ruth Prentice had the unenviable task of stepping into someone else's shoes at short notice to design the book. Our thanks go to her and to Sarah Bloxham, a patient and an unfailingly good humoured editor at Collins & Brown. Thanks also to Patricia Still of London Diary Publications Ltd for casting a vigilant eye over the galleys.

It is impossible to thank adequately two dear friends. Not only have books written by Felix Barker and Peter Jackson been invaluable but both have also given me the benefit of their encyclopaedic knowledge of London. It was at Peter's suggestion I undertook the text and he has willingly looked up answers to innumerable questions posed over the telephone at odd hours. Felix, forever full of ideas, read the manuscript and encouraged me, not always successfully, to keep on a straight and narrow road whenever I got sidetracked by some irrelevancy. Their help has been much appreciated.